Urban Politics
The Political Culture Of Gangs

Rodrigo Garcia Bernal

Bloomington, IN  Milton Keynes, UK

authorHOUSE®

AuthorHouse™
1663 Liberty Drive, Suite 200
Bloomington, IN 47403
www.authorhouse.com
Phone: 1-800-839-8640

AuthorHouse™ UK Ltd.
500 Avebury Boulevard
Central Milton Keynes, MK9 2BE
www.authorhouse.co.uk
Phone: 08001974150

This book is a work of non-fiction. Unless otherwise noted, the author and the publisher make no explicit guarantees as to the accuracy of

First published by AuthorHouse 8/14/2006

ISBN: 1-4259-5298-4 (sc)

Printed in the United States of America
Bloomington, Indiana

This book is printed on acid-free paper.

Dedicated to:

John Highland, Brian Highland, Alfonso Jacobo, John Jacobo, Jose Ramos, Freddy Sanchez, Tony Martinez, and David Robles.

Special Thanks to:

Susana Bernal, Belisario Garcia, Cipriano Romo, Olivia Romo, Rick Garcia, Mark Garcia, Pete Chavez, Arnold Llerena, David Robles, Eddie Garcia, Israel Mosqueda, Peter Davalos, Alfredo Garcia, Tony Martinez, Angelica Rosales, Hasmik Geghamyan, Pablo Garcia, Lai Tran, Alex Espinosa, Mary Lang, Martin Rivas, David Rosales, and Rachel Romero.

Contents

Prologue

Los Angeles County is made up of eighty eight incorporated cities that have formed and merged legally into the county corporation. They have a city hall, however, not all of the incorporated cities have an official city seal or a chamber of commerce, and many of these cities are either chartered or general-law cities.

The difference between a chartered city and a general law city is that a chartered city has a written document similar to a constitution that grants the city legal powers and jurisdiction, and a general-law city has an unwritten constitution that is based on general principles and customs.

There are also, forty unincorporated communities and forty seven unincorporated areas within Los Angeles County without a city hall, chamber of commerce, official seal, are not general-law or chartered cities, and they have not merged legally into the county corporation.

Additionally, the city of Los Angeles is the largest municipality within the county corporation and it houses ninety-one communities/areas within its boundary which are divided into regional blocs. The regional blocs include: San Fernando Valley (thirty communities), Westside/Beach/ Los Angeles International Airport or LAX (seventeen communities), Downtown/Central Los Angeles (twenty-one communities), Northeast Los Angeles (ten communities), South Los Angeles/

South Central (eight communities), and the Harbor Area, which has five communities. Lastly, there are another thirty five communities/areas within incorporated cities other than the city of Los Angeles. (L.A. County Almanac)

Correspondingly, there are more than four hundred street gangs within the Los Angeles County jurisdiction that have adopted the boundaries and territory within the incorporated cities and the unincorporated communities. They do not have a city hall, chamber of commerce, or official city seal; however they are all general law communities that operate under general principles and customs. These general law communities have the same function as a city or municipality: they are a center of population, commerce, and culture of some significant size and importance. These general law communities have not and will never merge legally into the county corporation. They do adhere to the division of boundaries and regional blocs that make up the Los Angeles County and the City of Los Angeles. Many of these street gang organizations operate within an incorporated city's boundaries: however, there are numerous communities and areas within these jurisdictions that proliferated in the 1970's, 80's, and 90's in an effort to resist the annexation of a larger street gang organization to remain autonomous.

Los Angeles County's cosmopolitan population makes it a unique and highly distinct global region with an attractive social and cultural landscape; however, the inequality and economic gap directly contribute to its paradoxical identity. The economic gap is so egregious that in many unincorporated communities, areas, and municipalities, the socio- economic status and the standard of living of its citizenry is comparable to that of third world countries. For example, the University of

Southern California, which is one of the most prestigious, elite, and expensive universities in the world, is surrounded by one of the poorest neighborhoods in the county. The demographics of the community are mostly made up of low-income blacks, Hispanics, and recent immigrants. On the other hand, the majority of the student body at the university comes from white, middle-class suburbs throughout the country. The chances of local residents attending the university are quite slim.

Another example, lies within the Culver City jurisdiction, where a local unincorporated community has been abandoned by local city officials and has been annexed by the City of Los Angeles. Located within the Westside regional bloc of the City of Los Angeles, the Mar Vista Gardens Housing Project, is home to mostly low-income Hispanics and recent immigrants from Mexico. A five minute drive east of the state-sponsored subsidized community are million dollar homes. A five minute drive to the west is Marina Del Rey, which is one of the most affluent communities within the county surrounded by the harbor and the beach cities. All around the housing project are expensive homes and Hollywood studio production companies.

Another unique example, lies within the Westside/Beach/LAX Airport jurisdiction. It is the community of Lennox, which is surrounded by one of the busiest and largest airports in the world, the aerospace industry, and private organizations such as Raytheon and Northrop. The community of Lennox serves as a cultural hub of the Westside regional bloc in that it appears to be the only area within the jurisdiction that looks like it has been taken out of a third world country and has been strategically placed in the middle of beach city suburbs.

The citizens of Lennox are mostly of Hispanic origin and recent immigrants, they have one of the lowest income levels per capita within the county, and many cannot speak English and have low educational attainment levels. The community has a high crime rate with little police response and involvement. The citizens do not get to vote on city measures and ordinances that affect their day to day lives. There is a high rate of teenage pregnancy and a lack of affordable housing. A simple drive through the focal street within the community would make you believe you were driving through Tijuana, Mexico. The streets are surrounded by liquor stores, taco stands, barber shops, carnicerias, small grocery stores, bakeries, strip clubs, prostitution, and street vendors selling: ice cream, corn on the cob, tacos, tamales, fruit, hot dogs, and pork rinds.

Appropriately, the community has been nicknamed "Little T.J." by local and adjacent residents because of its close resemblance to goods and services provided in Tijuana, Mexico. The architecture used to build some of the elementary schools resembles prisons, the fences are iron bars, the school colors are of a dull, grayish hue, few visible street signs identify a school crossing, and there are no speed bumps to reduce the speed of traffic in school zones. It is a poverty-stricken community with a high density level that renders serious traffic during school hours where narrow streets make it impractical to pick up children. Some schools, in fact, are located adjacent to adult video stores, strip clubs, and visible prostitution.

Many of the residents in the unincorporated community of Lennox provide low-skilled wage labor to the LAX Airport and the surrounding affluent neighborhoods. They are employed in: waste management, janitorial services, cooks, fast foods servers, maids, housekeepers, babysitters, truck/delivery drivers, ramp agents, mechanics, and many other essential jobs that directly contribute to the economy of the nation, state, and county. However, many are discriminated against. They are largely ignored by law enforcement, and they have no political representation. The private institutions surrounding the community are not reflective of the citizenry. Lennox lacks affordable housing and lacks social and public programs. Its depressed wages do not seem to fit within the context of a first world nation with a vibrant economy in a prestigious region of Los Angeles County. This phenomenon and social dichotomy is directly related to the economic gap between the rich and poor and causes social/economic/cultural depression, anxiety and alienation. Poverty-stricken, high density, and overpopulated immigrant communities are synonymous with gang activity. Gang activity is a way to cope with all the social conditions that are experienced within those jurisdictions. The escapism that gangs provide extends to drug and alcohol abuse, promiscuity, violence, crime, extortion, drug dealing, urban terrorism, prison life, and recidivism. Gang culture is a way to deal with the social paradox of existing in a world where the "American Dream" seems impossible to young Latino adolescents who cannot match up to their white counterparts, but have a value system different from their immigrant parents. This book will examine Hispanic street gang organizations in the Los Angeles County, the unique phenomenon of the Beach/LAX Airport/ Westside regional bloc, and assess the political culture of gangs including the jurisdiction of Lennox.

Chapter 1: Social Contract

"The state of nature is anarchic; it is a constant state of war of all against all. Human beings are in constant conflict between desires and power because the need to pursue those desires and power conflicts with that of others'. There is no guarantee that they will secure that which they covet in the future, so they pursue what they covet immediately, which means they must secure those desires and power at another's expense." (Hobbes) Law enforcement agencies and legislation are created to hinder those desires and potential abuse of power by the more cunning and skillful; therefore, the war of all against all is sanctioned into policies and procedures that fall within judicial regulations. Yet, even with legitimate authority in the form of law enforcement and city councils, those in the subterranean street life are usually ignored and victimized by law enforcement. They have no political representation, thus they operate under different laws. Those citizens who are disenfranchised are living in an anarchic state because there is no respect for recognized legal authority; therefore they have succumbed to lawlessness.

In the concrete jungle where there is no law, there is no justice or injustice, so everyone provides sanctuary for themselves and protects their families by buying guns, locking doors, fencing yards, putting bars on windows, installing surveillance cameras and motion lights, and having guard dogs. They are in a state of war because they are competing for scarce resources in the form of desires and power. The war of all against all is to protect themselves from the fear of danger and violent death, and to pursue their desires and power even though it conflicts with that of others'. The hoodlums, dissidents, troublemakers, thieves, criminals, and drug dealers are in a constant state of war of all against all and living in an anarchic state of nature. It is from this state of nature that they come together to pursue their self-preservation in the form of a social contract because they fear the constant war of all against all.

In the study of sociology, a term used to describe the competition for scarce resources in the form of over consumption and proliferation of material possessions is called "catching up with the Joneses." In urban working class neighborhoods there is no escaping this same phenomenon because of the proximity of affluence and the overwhelming advertisements that subconsciously affect the psyche into believing that more is better. There is the need for a new consumer product and the consistent reinforcement that without a surplus of paper currency one is insignificant.

Most Hispanic neighborhoods in the Los Angeles County are made up of working class immigrants who champion financial stability and try to improve their socio-economic status by joining the rat race, having a hard-working ethic, occasionally participating in the political process, paying property taxes, and buying a new vehicle. Large portions of the immigrant population come from rural towns in Mexico and Central America and have difficulty adjusting to an urban metropolis that helps develop a more global perspective and also detaches people from their communities simultaneously.

Because of the influence of affluence, these people somewhat adopt the ideology of the prevalent economic gap and begin to participate in the "catching up with the Garcia's (Joneses)" paradigm with the same competitive fervor as does the rest of the dominant population. Many see an opportunity through the constant flow of drugs, criminal activities such as burglary and battery, intimidation through extortion, and other unconventional methods they can capitalize on and improve their socio-economic status. It is through these alternative ways of financing luxury and material possessions, increasing their reputations through fear and intimidation, and protecting themselves from outsiders while maintaining peace within community boundaries that create a social contract.

When a social contract has been established through necessity, the 3 P's are always fundamental principles for legitimate creation and involvement. They include: peace, prosperity, and protection. Peace is necessary to eliminate hostilities and disagreements, and to establish civic order amongst its members. It is necessary for a social contract to have prosperity so that the citizens can flourish with material wealth and possessions, and pursue financial independence free from impediments. Lastly, protection is necessary from foreign invasion, intruders, domestic disputes, and any other social factors that can contribute to injury and harm. (Hobbes) The main reason to join the social contract is to have self-preservation in an anarchic concrete jungle that is controlled by lawlessness.

The social contract puts together informal mutual covenants that the participants can adhere to and secure their peace, prosperity, and protection. Those who do not join the social contract, must continue living in constant fear of danger and violent death because the social contract provides peace, prosperity, and protection to only those who have succumbed to the mutual covenants and agreements. The continuity of fear is extended to those citizens who do not join the social contract because it does not provide security to those outside of the social contract, thus, they are now open targets and become terrorized by gang members. The social contract is ratified through social norms and customs, making it traditional gang culture. It becomes legitimized and recognized by the consent of its members, law enforcement, citizens, politicians, and the media. Those who join the social contract lose their natural freedom of existence. They now succumb to customs and traditions that are not natural, however, in giving up some sovereignty, they gain security, civic freedom, and an unlimited right to do as they please. The social contract provides members with unlimited liberties that are absent of external impediments (license to kill), but because of the significant presence of actual law enforcement agencies, gang members conduct their day to day activities clandestinely.

The social contract creates a collective body of those individuals who are willing to risk their lives to preserve it, defend it, and fight for its honor against any opposition and foreign invasion. The social contract adopts boundaries created by government agencies and gives it a name usually adopted by the actual city or the unincorporated community. It also adopts real estate principles and adheres to the unwritten law of the right of first occupancy. They do not use bundles of rights, grant deeds, or security agreements to hold legal title, yet they "post up" (loiter) in different locations throughout their boundaries including dead ends, main avenues, small streets, parks, corner intersections, and alleys. They execute the right of first occupancy by "posting up" in certain locations that become their cornerstones for commerce (drug trade) and those areas become real property. They do not occupy territory with legal authority, yet they claim and occupy territory with fierce conviction, thus becoming usurpers, which then becomes the basic authority for the social contract and street gang intimidation. Because the name of the social contract has absolute authority and sovereignty, the name of the city, street, or unincorporated community is usually chosen to represent its members and is than publicly displayed in the form of graffiti and vandalism to demonstrate their significance. These locations that they have chosen to "post up" at become focal points of interest to its actual members, foreign rivals, political officials, law enforcement agencies, and the media.

Members of the social contract have so much love and respect for the sovereign that they tattoo their bodies with the name of their gang or social contract i.e. Lennox or Venice, thus demonstrating to everyone that their sovereign has absolute authority. The members of the social contract will usually not do anything that is contrary or conflicts with the original agreements of the social contract, thus any behavior such as renouncing membership (getting jumped out), switching allegiance, or not defending its honor (ranking out) usually results in denouncement and consequences.

Because the social contract is meant to maximize utility and provide the greatest good for the greatest amount, private interests are secondary and sometimes conflicting. The social contract is meant to secure group strength and power, make rights invincible, and make war upon hostile territories, instead of allowing its members to remain in an uncertain and precarious situation. (Rousseau) A paradox exists with this phenomenon because the joining members gain peace, prosperity, and protection within their boundaries, but they now become vulnerable to the enemies of the sovereign they did not have before. Signs of good governance of the sovereign can be witnessed when its members voluntarily increase and multiply in size, yet some sovereigns coerce its citizens, oblige covenants, and impose a belief system. The latter becomes somewhat of an imperialist sovereign that establishes colonies in other territories and implements administration over great distances. In the Los Angeles County, the 18th St. gang is the most expansive sovereign as it has established colonies throughout foreign territories, yet it is the least cohesive. There are significant disagreements within its leadership, and they are one of the most hated sovereigns within the county corporation. This is an interesting observation because residency in a certain location does not automatically indicate consent to that sovereign. Because they do not acknowledge that sovereign's authority, they now become foreigners within that territory. Moreover, it must also be noted that in rare occasion's siblings join opposing social contracts that have extreme adversarial relations, thus they are complete enemies on the streets, however; there is no general contributing factor to this phenomenon and it must be assessed on a case-by-case basis.

The same is true for sovereigns that refuse the annexation of a larger street gang and resist the colonization of its members in order to remain autonomous. Some smaller sovereigns that lie within the boundaries of a larger street gang fluctuate between creating peace and making war with the larger street gang depending on diplomatic relationships they have established with each other, or enemies they have in common. An example is with the Lennox 13 street gang, which has a large membership population in comparison to smaller street gangs such as Tepa (taken from a small rural town in Guadalajara, Mexico called Tepatitlan where its founders originated from) and MXP (Mexican Power, the name was used to demonstrate nationalism and solidarity), yet Tepa has become a significant rival despite its close proximity. The main reason is that Tepa gang members became separatists in order to resist domination and have self-determination. Many of those Tepa gang members went to the same elementary schools, and junior high school as did the Lennox gang members, but somewhere between their curriculums they decided that their liberties were being undermined by the social contract in Lennox. The result was their own social contract called Tepa, which resulted in naked aggression and hostility, denouncement, and expulsion from basic Lennox boundaries, with the exception of a few streets within a two mile radius, and the basic freedom to attend a different high school. This significant demarcation resulted in street warfare between the two sovereigns that still exists today. On the other hand, MXP started as a nationalist organization that transcended boundaries and established peaceful relations with members of different sovereigns. However, over time they became more aggressive with known Lennox adversaries, they hung out in Lennox territories, went to the same schools, maintained close and friendly relationships, and sooner or later became co-opted into the larger street gang and became a competing faction. (See Ch. 13.)

Despite the significant hostilities, gang member murders, and constant street warfare, those who have joined the social contract are not real or natural enemies. They are only enemies because of circumstances and situational relations, thus they are participating in street warfare for the sake of the social contract and its authority. As was mentioned earlier, many of these gang members used to have friendly relations before they joined the social contract, yet once they joined the social contract they adopted the belief system that imposes a state of war amongst them. This means that they are only accidental enemies and that the state of war between them does not actually exist, it is a war of sovereigns and those gang members become soldiers and defenders of its honor.

Street warfare is a cyclical process that continues because the objective is to see the destruction of another sovereign, specifically if one protects the sovereign with weapons, because the social contract establishes a state of war against hostile territories and gives its members absolute authority to kill. If a gang member renounces his membership in a social contract, if he refuses or no longer wishes to defend the honor of that sovereign, or if he puts down his weapons used to defend the sovereign, he ceases to be an enemy and no longer should he be a target of hatred and aggression. Those that decide to renounce their membership in a social contract return to a civilian lifestyle and must be respected by adversaries because the right to kill them no longer exists, and they should be allowed to pursue a life that is free from impediments such as street warfare, hostility and aggression, and disciplinary action. (Rousseau)

Chapter 2: Secret Societies

All social contracts within street gang organizations have established their regime as a secret society. All secret societies throughout the world possess esoteric information whether it is technological, political, economical, religious, operational, metaphysical, etc... and use it to their benefit. Street gang organizations possess economic and operational intelligence that is not available to all members of a society. Therefore, they possess a valuable commodity that becomes scarce and is only available through exclusive membership. Secret societies in Medieval Europe and Arabia were formed on subversive platforms and worked against established authorities to pursue their objectives and desires. (Parfrey) Some secret societies were formed to fight oppression and resisted tyrannical domination, such as the Freemasons, thus, gang members who have worked cooperatively for the protection of the community and fought oppression and domination can be said to have formed a secret society based on subversive platforms. (Daraul) By resisting the status-quo and oppression, street gang organizations formed a secret society through a social contract that protected their general law community and became subversive units that operated throughout the Los Angeles County. The ability of these secret societies to proliferate quickly was due to its very nature of secrecy and mysticism. This invokes curiosity and confusion in most people, thus the gang becomes an antisocial organization that echoes fear and intimidation, and increases membership among impressionable adolescents.

In forming secret societies, members create an organizational culture that establishes norms, behaviors, customs, dress codes, and mannerisms. Dress codes are quite common in secret societies, such as the Assassins that wore white robes and red boots, or the Witchcraft cults that wore black cloaks, and so gang members also have their own dress code. (Daraul) The dress code symbolizes uniformity, equality and is to reflect a battle dress posture amongst the members unless they have grand masters or high priests who might wear a more symbolic outfit with different colors that is usually obtained through seniority and leadership skills. In secret society gangs, the veteran members who have become more interested in fiscal policy, administration, and implementation are considered the high priests or grand masters because of their seniority, their work in congress, or their leadership skills and wear less conspicuous clothing.

Most gang members come from low-income working class families and as a result, they shop at local swap meets and military surplus stores. This, in-turn, offers gang members the convenience of purchasing a uniform which reflects gang attire while offering the benefits of being able to buy such garb within close proximity and affordability to their respective turfs. For example, traditional gang attire often includes: inexpensive sneakers such as Converse (Chuck Taylor), Nike (Cortez), and Vans (late 70's style slip-on) styles. House slippers commonly referred to as zig-zags, Chinese shoes, boulevards, or *chanclas* (sandals), also represent a further extension of this. This style of footwear is often accessorized with long white tube socks, and oversized shorts, which are usually cut-off. The popular name brands within these accessories are working class clothing brands such as Ben Davis, Dickies, or Levi's, which are oversized and commonly referred to as *baggy* within the social norm. Traditional belts included a letter buckle usually with the beginning letter of the gang or the nickname adopted by each specific gang member. Also, oversized plain white t-shirts, polo shirts (Le Tigre), button-downed Pendleton's, hooded or v-neck sweaters, plain black jackets, and sports jerseys. Dark colored baseball caps, gloves (commonly referred to as brownies within gang circles), beanies, thick mustaches and beards, little facial hair and short hair or a bald head are all customs adopted by gang member secret societies. One important item to note here is that throughout the greater Los Angeles County, gang members wear Los Angeles Dodgers and Raiders sports gear. They do so because such dark, solid colors reflect a strong message of aggression and patriotism towards the common masses. Coincidentally, these groups (street gangs and sport teams) often exist within a constant competitive state of warring nature (albeit the latter is performed through publicly sanctioned sporting events). Ultimately, such dress code symbolizes the resistance of the status-quo, the overt display of membership to foreign intruders, passerby's, and, officials in law enforcement. This is done in order to produce fear and intimidation by publicly displaying the attire of those in urban warfare within the concrete jungle.

Secret societies speak in code, use signs and symbols, develop handshakes, and inflict self-mutilation that become customs and norms. Secret societies in Europe were trained in languages to disguise clandestine activities and objectives, similarly, secret society gangs speak in code as they have developed a simple, yet unconventional dialect that includes English, Spanish, and slang that is not understood by the general population. They also use sign language to spell out their neighborhoods, or adopt a letter or combination of letters to identify their gang that becomes recognizable to other gang members and observers. Handshakes are commonly used, usually with a clever sequence of shakes and then ending with their main sign, which is also traditional in other secret societies. Because of their strange and abnormal customs, their utter lack of respect for law enforcement, their undesirable and terrorizing activities, and their subversive nature, they gain an air of mystery wrapped around a bad reputation that leaves the community shocked and disgusted.

Traditional symbols of secret society gangs include the number 13 after each gang to represent the 13th letter of the alphabet. (Most secret societies use numerology in general) which is M for Mexican, graffiti-style writing which would be pictographs, blue bandanas that represent the South Side (Southern California) as opposed to the North Side (Northern California). This custom began by prison authorities who distributed blue/red railroad handkerchiefs to the different factions. Additionally, automatic weapons and Catholic figures that symbolize how they live by the sword and spirit, like the Knights Templar, are cherished gang symbols. (Most Hispanic gangs have Catholic leanings because the majority of Mexicans are of Catholic descent.)

As the name suggests, the Castrators of Russia used self-mutilation as a way of achieving mystical insight. (Daraul) Tribal societies in New Zealand and Australia used tattooing, markings, and piercings to reach a state of excitement, ritual, or a symbol of hierarchical structure. These methods of self-mutilation become a cultural norm for members of secret societies that must be able to have a high tolerance and threshold for pain to demonstrate their courage and fearlessness. Secret society gangs use similar self-mutilation methods to maintain rituals and norms that become part of the organizational culture such as tattooing, markings, and piercings. Common tattoos amongst secret society gangs in Los Angeles County include: 3 dots in the form of a triangle to represent "mi vida loca" (my crazy life), the Los Angeles Dodgers symbol, which is a connected L.A. to symbolize patriotism, a Mongolian warrior/jinni or Aztec warriors that symbolize courage and fearlessness, Aztec calendars and pyramids that represent ethnic demographics, old English writing to represent the neighborhood, and last name, clique (political party) or regional bloc. Usually the number 13 is incorporated after the neighborhood in handwriting, old English, or block letters, song dedications usually from old school love songs (oldies) such as Smile Now Cry Later called a chain, which is normally a chain around the neck, and other symbols that have become representative of the lifestyle including; jokers, clowns, lowrider vehicles, prison bars, fearsome-looking mascots, devils, and girls with spaghetti-looking hair. Also common are portraits of the Virgin Mary, Jesus Christ, praying hands with a rosary around them, and crosses that suggest a strong Catholic background, although devils and clowns could exist in the same collage usually exhorting duality. Although pierced ears, tongues, lips, and eyebrows are common in secret societies, the symbolic tattooing is used to maintain the status-quo amongst the participating members and those with the most, biggest, or most noticeable tattoos are usually looked upon as the most courageous and fearless.

Many secret societies had religious objectives or included religious-magical rituals to attain a state of excitement. Secret society gangs use a monstrous combination of Catholic religion, paganism, and primitive superstitions that were incorporated into their symbolic tattooing and thought process in general. Two of the most notorious gangs in the Downtown/ Central Los Angeles regional bloc are MS (Mara salva trucha) and 18th St., which are rumored to be satanic devil worshippers that revere evil, terrorize and murder victims with absolute brutality, and are sometimes considered sinister cults that practice black magic and sacrifice. Many of those members come from civil war-torn countries including; El Salvador, Nicaragua, and Honduras, many of whom have witnessed dead and decayed bodies in the public streets, heartless executions, and consistent brutality. As these citizens are displaced from their countries and come to the United States, a new type of street warfare exists in the urban metropolis. Different types of pressure-groups exist wherever humanity congregates, thus many become absorbed by the social contract and secret societies to maintain their survival and protection of the community. Law enforcement agencies, state, and local prisons are overwhelmed with the density of inmates. Therefore, they have taken steps to deport illegal immigrants that are arrested for gang/criminal activities and are than sent back to Central America or Mexico. This latter fact has caused a nationwide panic in those countries because of their sinister nature, rapid expansion, and the exportation of street gangs in their countries. (See Ch 10.)

Most secret societies adopt rituals that include initiation rites, exclusive membership, and fiduciary agreements and obligations. In general secret societies, oath taking, vows of silence and secrecy, adopting principals, and imposing exclusive membership promote myth and ritual with special meaning to its participants designating organizational norms. In secret society gangs, the initiation rites usually include a jump-in (beat down), adoption of a pseudonym, choosing of a clique (partisanship), and in some cases a criminal act of violence to demonstrate loyalty and fearlessness. Under exclusive membership, many gang members have a probationary period to demonstrate loyalty and courage, some are examined prior to initiation rites, some have a trainee program where an individual actually hangs out and participates in clandestine activities without going through the initiation rites, and many are tested randomly for loyalty and courage. Fiduciary agreements and obligations include; upholding the social contract and defending its honor regardless of whoever denounces it, not retreating in battle regardless of the odds against them, demonstrating fearlessness and barbaric ruthlessness, embracing all ages, not leave the organization after the initiation process, and enforcing a strict policy of not snitching or betraying a fellow member. Defecting from the gang, retrieving in defeat, ranking out (not upholding the social contract), and showing fear can lead to severe penalties and repercussions, however, betraying a fellow member usually results in their own type of jurisprudence, which usually involves execution.

Many secret societies develop certain behaviors and mannerisms that can sometimes be considered tasteless and harmful such as debauchery and induced drug use and alcohol consumption to produce ecstasy and enhanced mental states. Gang members are known for their excesses of debauchery, fornication with loose women, and indiscriminate sexual relations. Orgiastic drumming is common in tribal secret societies as it can also be witnessed in modern street gang secret societies at local parties and hang outs which would include freaking (stimulating dances that involve vulgar sexual perversion), and promiscuity that produces player-status (honorable reputation including that of a lady's man). Although debauchery and drug/ alcohol use is not necessarily expected and imposed, it is heavily encouraged in pressure groups such as these and even becomes ritual for some; however, it could also be viewed as an excuse for licentiousness.

Because these pressure groups are consistently engaged in street warfare and criminal activities, the need to experiment and induce labor (put in work) through drug/alcohol abuse is quite normal and becomes customary. It is common for young, vulnerable adolescents to try to impress the grand masters and high priests, their subordinates, and there contemporaries (peers). So, many rely on alcohol or drug use for ecstasy that is produced by excitatory methods followed by manipulation of the mind. Some of these participants use the drugs to produce enhanced mental states, while many use them just to get high, because of ritual, or to simply escape from reality, thus leading to drug addiction. Fear and intimidation are such significant factors in pressure groups, especially in secret society gangs, because one single criminal activity can cost the member his life. For example, going to jail or getting killed are common consequences. The philosophy of the gang is that one man or group of men can have absolute power over another's decision-making authority.

Adopting surnames is common in secret societies because of its very nature of secrecy, the ease of identification amongst themselves, decipherable hieroglyphics on walls that only some can recognize, and a personification of something outside of themselves. For example, some secret societies adopt animal names to personify an animal because of their characteristic that cannot be done by any common man or because of their resemblance to the animal. Some of these names include: Grizzly, Cricket, and Vamp. Other names are adopted because of the way the individuals look such as; Sporty, Baby-face, and Shady. Various names are adopted because of the reverence for evil such as; Wicked, Diablo, and Spooky. Descriptive names are adopted because the individuals behave a certain way such as; Wacky, Rascal, or Boxer. Select names are taken from cartoon characters such as; Boo-Boo, Scrappy, Dopey, and Spanky. And still others are taken from old school songs (oldies) such as; Puppet, Stranger, and Shy-boy. After so many names have been used, they start to become a bit innovative and unconventional to avoid the recycling of names, but the actual process itself has become an organizational norm.

Secret societies engage in fraternal behavior that is also linked to liberty and equality. By developing a fraternity masked behind a secret society and social contract, the experiences that are shared, bonds the members rather closely. The rituals, norms, customs, mannerisms, and behaviors are so commonplace, that when they are altered, the entire group becomes disillusioned. They have succumbed to the organizational culture also called "groupthink." Sharing experiences that include: drug/alcohol rituals, scars from the battle zone, events and scenes from the historical street warfare, close encounters of death and violence, time spent in prison, criminal activities, nights of debauchery and sexual perversion, paying homage to friends that have been murdered, and other such factors that bond people together allows for the fraternal state of mind that has developed in secret society gangs. Over the years, they become nostalgic and talk about the "good old days" and recall how they were able to progress through cooperation.

Secret societies are community oriented as they have stressed the community over the individual and terrorized the community by usurping the neighborhood, gaining recruits and converts by appealing to sensationalism, glorified fighting/violence/killing, and dedicated themselves to fraternity, money, and power. The fraternal behavior helps to develop a sense of equality with individuality because the objective is the same, (to defend the community), and the liberty is expressed with the licentiousness and ability to pursue criminal activities at nobody's expense.

Arkon Daraul maintains that, "the uniqueness of the true secret society is that certain aspects of human thought which are particularly compelling are combined to train and maintain the efforts of a group of people to operate in a certain direction." The true objective of the secret society is to develop a collective body of individuals that subject themselves voluntarily to an organizational culture that has absolute sovereignty over their decision-making authority. Secret societies everywhere have similar objectives including: the desire for power, love of mystery, sense of being someone special, sense of belonging, and the feeling that one will gain something extraordinary by membership. (Daraul) Most law enforcement agencies and non-participants believe that because they only persecute each other, they should be left to their own devices, however, this type of thinking changed when innocent victims were murdered, and the criminal activities started becoming rampant. As secret societies gangs became larger in size and membership was proliferating, the need to develop a more central authority and to separate into factions as cliques became necessary. The next chapter will examine cliques as political parties and how partisanship becomes a significant role in policy implementation and public administration.

Chapter 3: Political Parties

In order to have central authority and carry out administrative efforts, a hierarchical structure is needed to maintain stability. Those that make up the central authority in a hierarchical structure exercise some type of authority and try to carry out policies; however their opinions or paradigms can cause a conflict of interest. Because the difference in opinions causes division, factions develop and the centralized type of governance becomes polarized. Political parties have developed throughout history because of this phenomenon and the governance of a street gang organization which has become a general-law community with central authority is no exception. As street gang organizations increase in size, they begin to develop cliques that soon begin to adopt certain names and ideologies that become representative of that group of individuals. When young adolescents begin the initiation process and start to adopt the rituals, customs, and behaviors, they must also choose partisanship and decide which faction/paradigm/clique they identify with and register themselves with that party. The larger the organization, the more cliques/parties emerge, however, there are several small street gang organizations that do not have any parties and are highly centralized, and some small gangs only have a two-party system. Bowman maintains that, "parties function as umbrella organizations that shelter loose coalitions of relatively like-minded individuals." This is true for street gang organizations as well because their different cliques are the umbrella organizations that shelter like-minded individuals that create or join certain cliques based on identification, geography, or social-economic status. Some parties are created because of straight partisan differences; some are created around the age of its members, some because of geographical locations, and some because of social class differences. Party identification is sometimes created before an individual registers with that party, after they have joined the social contract, and sometimes members switch allegiance because their interests are not parallel with that of the parties or their interests have shifted to another party.

The ideological spectrum recognizes five ideologies as the most common and most political parties in the United States are loosely created around these broad ideas. Looking at the ideological spectrum from left to right, each ideology will be shortly summarized and identified as follows:

Radical- at the left of the spectrum considered leftists, willing to overthrow central authority through violence or revolution, large government involvement, and using extreme methods for change.

Liberal- Government should promote social welfare of the population, want gradual change within the current system and status quo, and reject hostile takeover of government.

Moderate- Share views with liberals and conservatives, tolerant of others' views and do not have extreme views of their own, and stand with different groups from issue to issue.

Conservative- Traditional views and maintaining the status quo, cautious about adopting new policies especially if significant change will take place, and less government involvement.

Reactionary- At the end of the spectrum considered the extreme right, want to go back to the good old days, and use repressive force to achieve goals. (www.usnewsclassroom. com)

Many street gang organizations follow the spectrum inadvertently and create factions that represent the different positions and issues. When an impressionable individual decides to join the social contract, he is subconsciously making a decision to join a clique based on social and economic issues while considering such factors as government change, flexibility, government involvement, and repression. When joining a smaller gang that does not have party identification because it does not exist, such factors are not considered and membership is strictly based on the absolute authority of that sovereign. Street gang organizations with political parties hold their party and sovereign as a dual governing authority, however it is sometimes mixed and sometimes identification is stronger with the party rather than the sovereign and vice versa.

The Lennox street gang organization will be assessed in this chapter including its cliques as political parties and as a multiparty system showing how they fit into the ideological spectrum. There are more political parties in this organization including: Tiny Locos, Midgets, MxP's, and Hollywood Bandits, yet those below resemble the ideological spectrum much closer and will be considered major parties, while the former will be considered minor parties.

Jokers- on the far left of the spectrum, considered subversives and unconventional, willing to overthrow existing authority and go against the status quo, use violence and revolution to implement change.

Night-owls- central government should promote welfare of all of the members, gradual change is desirable, and do not want violent takeover of central authority.

Peewee Locos- side with those on the right and left on certain issues, tolerate views of all cliques and no extreme views of their own.

Tokers-traditional views of street life culture and maintain status quo, skeptical of new policies that will introduce unconventional ideas, and less government involvement.

Winos- at the end of the spectrum considered the far right, want to use repressive force to produce change, and want to take the neighborhood back to the good old days.

Each political party within the Lennox street gang has a central committee that is the decision-making body for the clique and they select nominees to represent their party within the central authority by caucus or informal small meetings. Once a representative is chosen, he will serve as the liaison between the political party and the central authority and usually has good diplomacy skills, is well-liked, and has demonstrated good leadership skills. The central committee is self-appointed and the nominees are not chosen by the constituency or the rest of the clique, yet they are hand-picked by committee incumbents, which is an elitist unit that usually has a party agenda and seems to be well organized and revered by its constituency. (Often times the representative chosen will be from the central committee.) The constituency will be considered here as the rest of the members of the party that do not have the "requisite experience, stability, and judgment, to play a full role in the political life of the community." (Jillson) Only those that belong to the committee have collective decision-making authority and their power is exercised through acquiescence, however, there is room for climbing up the social ladder from the constituent level through demonstration of courageous efforts and close relationships with those in the committee. Those in the committee can benefit from the spoils of politics including: access to public funds, high-level political offices, government contracts including assassinations, and other various opportunities. Similar to other government bodies, street gang organizations are not above corruption, scandals, and patronage.

The political parties in Lennox also have a headquarters where they hold formal/informal meetings, caucuses, secret society rituals, capital intensive programs (drug selling), and other miscellaneous activities. When the central committees choose a representative and send him off as an appointed official serving as a liaison between the party and central authority, he represents these districts, which are the headquarters. These will include: the Jokers at Buford Avenue (Joker Town), the Night-owls at the Mansel dead-end (The Nest), the Peewee Locos at Felton, the Tokers on The Ave, and the Winos at Tumbas. Although the headquarters is mostly party-oriented, individuals from other parties/cliques are welcome and many times encouraged to travel through as transients or permanents to others' headquarters. It is not rare when members from other parties spend most of their time at a foreign headquarters serving ambassadorships, establishing diplomatic relations, or simply having a better sense of fraternity with members of another party, which does not mean they are not loyal to their own party. On the contrary, those parties that host the ambassadors use this factor to enhance public opinion throughout the street gang organization, and the ambassadors get a better sense of belonging because their loyalty transcends borders.

However, this is not to say that there is not weak partisanship; sometimes self-destructive behavior, weak partisanship, and dubious loyalty results in physical discipline at the constituency level because most parties are image-oriented. Self-destructive behavior in the form of drug abuse is ridiculed and frowned upon. Weak partisanship shows a weak party apparatus, and dubious loyalty can be considered cynical, hence physical discipline in the form of beat-downs and verbal reprimands are implemented because image and respect is everything. Ambassadors can even sit at a central committee hearing, yet they cannot vote on policy implementation and other decisions that require a three-quarter's majority. Despite parties' headquarters and party loyalty, conventions are held on a regular basis on the main focal street in Lennox, which is Inglewood Avenue. Here they represent and uphold the social contract where all members interact, discuss, and lobby. They also host other street gang organizations with entertainment such as festivals and sports activities, which will be looked at in Chapter 12.

These political party organizations do not run a democratic process because they do not use open/closed/or blanket primaries, elections, initiatives, referendums, campaigns, or the civil service system to put their party in the majority, however, they are motivated to work together and try to obtain or remain in power. Moreover, they do use the recall to remove certain members from office either through convention where the citizenry is allowed to express their opinions, or by physical force.

For example, in 1995, the Lennox street gang organization had a representative of the conservative right, who was part of the central committee, and who had served long and numerous prison terms. He was big in stature, used repressive force amongst other gang members, and continuously subjugated subordinates to ridicule, taxation without representation, discipline, and forced labor. He would also hold council meetings at his party's headquarters and accuse other party members of extreme partisanship, sectarianism, dissent, and government polarization. The city council had tried neutralizing his coercive behavior and encouraged him and those in his party to use diplomatic means to interact with fellow gang members. Most of his constituency and party-members distanced themselves from him and did not support his repressive behavior. Yet, they feared him because of his reputation, size, and career. The city council held a private meeting and decided that a recall was necessary and leaked the information to the media and held a caucus at a neutral convention center, which was the Lennox Middle School. At the caucus, his repressive behavior had been documented and released for public scrutiny, and now he was being held accountable for his actions and was subjected to discipline and recall. His discipline was brutal and bloody, which left him hospitalized with broken bones. He was completely removed from public office, and he withdrew himself from the street gang organization.

The goal of the political party organization is to place some of its members at the central authority level, which has executive decision-making control and who is responsible for implementing and interpreting legislative policies that they can draft up or benefit from. Some of those policies will require multiparty consensus, thus parties compete to present alternative programs to the overall population on how to maintain security, opportunity, and progress. During conventions or appointments of political figures, the central committees that represent their constituency choose candidates that range from radical to reactionary on the ideological spectrum to represent the attitudes of their party and reflect the public mood. Political parties are a great way to maintain stability and competition for power because of a polarized and decentralized street gang organization; however factions can lead to extreme loyal opposition and dissent, unhealthy divisions within the public, difficult public administration, dubious public interest, and sometimes civil war.

Chapter 4: City Council Structure

After a street gang general law community has adopted a social contract, after it has established itself as a secret society antisocial organization, and after it has divided itself between competing factions, it must create stability and order through a governing structure to provide overall leadership. The members of the governing structure (also called shot-callers) must create a system that becomes their standard of operations and defines procedures in order to have a well (or not so well) functioning government. They do not draft up a charter or written constitution to outline their local government structure or their objectives, yet they do adopt some basic structures of a typical city council. As political parties (cliques) congregate at their headquarters and discuss the day-to-day issues amongst their party members. Social concerns that affect the well being of the citizenry must be addressed and communicated to higher levels of authority. The parties' central committees handle issues that affect party members and make decisions based on the well-being of their constituency; however, the central authority is responsible for discussing/debating issues and passing policies that affect the overall well-being of the entire street gang organization. Those that make up the central authority are the city council members and are chosen from the competing factions. Many adopt elitist theory behavior and believe they naturally possess leadership skills and can make better informed decisions, most serve on the central committees of their parties, and many have served prison terms, which amongst the citizenry yields some sort of respect, admiration, fear, and intimidation wrapped up in one neat package. Because fear and intimidation are such important factors in exercising power and authority, those gang members who possess extraordinary courage (down and crazy), barbaric ruthlessness (down to blast), some sort of seniority (older homies), and charismatic leadership skills, will eventually be considered for decision-making authority, or will assume leadership through self-appointment. In most street gang organizations, self-appointment is approved amongst peers, contemporaries, and subordinates after that gang member has returned from active duty in prison (see Chapter 7.) and news articles have been circulating through word of mouth about that individual's extraordinary accomplishments and efforts. This type of publicity is beneficial to that individual's reputation, because when he returns from a prison term, his authority is usually tacit and needs no consent. He warrants unlimited respect (which is another important factor in gang culture), and he can impose policies that are immediately enforced.

At the highest level of governance in a city council is the mayor, which has overall leadership, and executes policies for the entire community. A street gang organization has the same position without the official title and is usually considered the major shot-caller. Moreover, in actual political organizations the label is given to the person who occupies the position, but in a street gang organization it is the surname itself that renders the respect and admiration because an individual's name and reputation can carry a lot of weight. This is sometimes an elected official or a self-appointed position depending mostly on circumstance rather than structure. He is usually chosen from the city council, moves into the position immediately after serving a prison term, and has the luxury of chairing any meeting of any political party. According to Kearny and Bowman, city councils usually have four types of structures which include:

Mayor-council (strong mayor with lots of executive authority and limited authority to city council)

Weak-Mayor council (which limits mayor role to figurehead, host, or greeter, and serves ceremonial tasks such as public speaking and chairing meetings)

Council-Manager (strong city council that makes and executes policy)

City-commission form (in which commissioners make policy as members of the city's governing board)

In street gang organizations, the city commissioner seems to be the most popular form of government because the city council members can be both policymakers and policy executors serving as administrators and legislators and one commissioner is usually designated as the figurehead to preside over the city council meetings. Street gang organizations do not have enough members, revenues, and expertise to run an actual staff that separates administrative from legislative duties, thus the city commission form works best for them.

In the unincorporated community of Lennox and in other street gang organizations, it is not rare to have a mayoral figurehead run his administration like a dictatorship (mixed government) and enforce policies through coercion and repression. Often times the self-appointed dictator will serve a term in prison and return with Machiavellian intentions and execute policies through fear and intimidation, and deceive the citizenry through lies and deception. A dictator often has a small government and imposes high taxes so that those in the commission can benefit from a large share of the city's budget or allocated resources for themselves. The city council members will usually acquiesce to the policies of the mayor/dictator if they benefit from the spoils of politics, if not, serious divisions in government can result in succession and even civil war.

The city council members have a duty to their constituency and to their political party (if they represent a political party) and must pass or veto policies with their constituency in mind. The city councils usually hold weekly or monthly council meetings where they discuss and compromise issues in regards to policy, budget, and maintenance. There is usually an agenda and most record the minutes of the day and go back to their constituency and/or party and discuss it in greater detail with their central committees and sometimes their entire constituency. Citizens want to be governed well and feel like they have some involvement in the political process. Therefore, the challenge to the city council is to provide goods and services (weapons/drugs) on a timely manner, they must remain receptive to structural improvements, there should be tranquility among public officials, and they should allow for change within the government allowing for flexibility. Sometimes the city council can become disproportionate because a district or party might be underrepresented and a group of citizens can become disenfranchised resulting in factions and a high turnover rate or loss of membership.

A street gang organization can usually be easy to manage because the council members and the constituency come from the same socioeconomic stratum, they share the same political philosophy, and they are always homogenized urban communities. Most city councils in street gang organizations succumb to the elitist leadership theory in which a small group of individuals/ leaders exercise power and enjoy a strategic advantage in influencing government decisions. Because the mayor is the central authority figure, his ultimate task is to maintain the peace, prosperity, and protection amongst the citizenry and pass policies that reflect this philosophy, which will be discussed in Chapter 6.

Chapter 5: The Budget: Taxing and Spending

In order to continue maintenance in any organization, the allocation of monies is necessary for its existence. The way a street gang is organized with its city council, political parties, and central authority; budgeting principles are required to maintain sovereignty and protection from hostile aggression. The government is responsible for delivering goods and services in a timely manner; therefore it is the fiduciary duty of city council members and those with decision-making authority to provide those services so that the citizenry can uphold the social contract at all costs. Street gang organizations are in a constant state of street warfare, therefore defense spending becomes the largest portion of its allocation of resources. Street gang organizations adopt the principles of taxing, spending, and intergovernmental relations (with Congress/jail), and this in turn contributes to the political culture of gangs. Financing any organization can be an arduous task, so a street gang organization must introduce a budget cycle and examine its revenues and expenditures.

In the state of California, local governments rely on the state assembly for funding that has trickled down from the federal government to them. The federal government collects taxes from several sources, distributes monies to state governments, and the states distribute those monies to counties and local governments. This process is considered "intergovernmental relations" which government agencies and organizations rely on one another for resources. (Jillson) The same is true for street gang organizations; however the prison senate (congress/jail) is more dependent on street gang organizations and members on the outside to provide economic assistance. For obvious reasons, commerce and business is facilitated from the outside, therefore the prison senate collects taxes from the city councils on the outside and it becomes a good source of revenues for the Congress. It is rare for a sovereign street gang on the outside to refute the tax imposed by the Congress; however it did happen during the Treaty of the South with the Tax Revolt of the Marravilla gangs, which resulted in liquidation and catastrophe. (See Chapter 11)

Since most street gang organizations can collect from their own sources rather than the prison senate, the city councils are responsible for financing their own administrations. Whether the administration is liberal or conservative, taxing and spending principles revolve around commerce and defense spending because of the constant state of war. Most street gang organizations have a laissez-faire or hands-off economy with limited regulation. This basically means that individuals are allowed and encouraged to pursue business ventures, but can later be taxed at a higher level because of their ability to pay more, hence the regulation. Most city councils levy a progressive income tax in which an increase in their contribution is directly influenced by the percentage of their income. City council members promote entrepreneurship and business ideas in order to rely heavily on the personal income tax for revenues because it is the easiest to impose. Street gang administrations collect revenues from: individual, business/

corporate, general sales, property, transportation, and other miscellaneous taxes. Individual taxes can be collected from any members of the constituency that have a legal/ civilian job or from any gang member that is engaged in capital intensive programs (drug selling/ stealing cars). Business/ corporate taxes can be collected from any member that has established an actual business such as a sole proprietorship, partnership, or corporation and can contribute a larger portion due to his ability-to-pay. General sales taxes are imposed on any such products that can be purchased on the black market such as drugs, guns, and ammunition, and can be purchased above cost. Property taxes are collected from city councils on the outside as a means to protect its fellow members in jail from hostile aggression and paid to the prison senate. Those in jail are considered real and movable property and although it seems abstract, it is a good source of revenue for the congress. The transportation tax is imposed informally because instead of having a motor fuel and vehicle licensing fee, the city council mandates a contribution tax when a vehicle is commandeered for commerce, business, or war, the individual must surrender his vehicle for utilitarian purposes. There are other miscellaneous taxes, for example: Lennox gang members engage in tourism, which means they rob tourists because of the proximity of the airport, however miscellaneous taxes are usually regional and circumstantial.

After street gang organizations have collected revenues and levied taxes on the citizenry, it must spend those monies in areas where they can deliver more goods and services to the general pubic. The city councils impose a general income tax on political parties (if no political parties exist, individuals are taxed) and it is up to the central committee of the political party to collect those revenues from their constituency. The personal income tax is then collected by the central committees and distributed to the city council which in turn gets placed in a general or special fund. Monies for guns, drugs, ammunition, congress, and transportation go to the general fund, while monies for healthcare, funeral arrangements, and other miscellaneous items, which are also regional and circumstantial, go to the special fund. Street gang organizations have expenditures which include: housing and community development, public safety, defense spending, parks and recreation, healthcare, transportation, and culture/leisure. Housing and community development expenditures include rent, lease, or mortgage payments to homes or motels that provide drug traffic and contribute directly to the gross domestic product (GDP). Public safety expenditures include military defense spending on weapons, ammunition, and patrol units that observe the urban complex, like a neighborhood watch, to keep surveillance of possible intruders and foreign invasion. Parks and recreation expenditures include contributions to any events held at a local park including sporting events, barbecues, conventions, and secret society-type rituals. Healthcare expenditures include contributions to hospitalized patients and their families and contributions to funeral expenses, however the healthcare expenditures are arbitrary and subject to personal volunteerism, there is no state-sponsored healthcare program, and the burden usually lies with the victim's family. There are transportation expenditures including maintenance, gas, mileage, stealing/stripping vehicles (g-rides), and culture/ leisure expenditures including musical festivals, mega-sporting events, and typical conventions and parties. There are also miscellaneous expenditures including attorney fees and public contributions to congress members, yet this is also an arbitrary expenditure and usually based on the rapport the congressman has with certain members of his constituency.

In street gang organizations, the mayor proposes the budget to the city council based on projections and assessments, but they do not adhere to an actual budget cycle or a fiscal year. They do not have a Department of Finance that is an independent agency providing expert analysis on fiscal information; rather the budget is mostly dependent on the mayor's speculations. It is not a democratic process because taxing and spending procedures are not transparent and public officials cannot really be held accountable because there is no way to prove if an administration is in a deficit, or if they have a surplus. It is not a line item budget, which allows council members to veto specific lines from the budget proposal, but it does categorize expenditures and revenues by function and character. It does require a majority approval by the city council, it takes into consideration debt incurred, and it is particular about preventing expenditures from exceeding revenues. Although street gang organizations are affected by intergovernmental relations with the prison congress, most sovereign street gangs enjoy a substantial amount of autonomy and when constrained they must find a way to increase taxes from their available sources, however, the funding must be spent on goods and services demanded by the public and it should reflect policies that benefit the welfare of the populous. (Jillson)

Chapter 6: Types of Policies and Policy Implementation

The administrative structure of a complex organization is known as a bureaucracy, and administration is "the nonpartisan profession and application of means to achieve public administration." (Jillson) Therefore, in street gang organizations, the bureaucracy is made up of the city council members who are responsible for legislative and administrative duties because they cannot separate both functions and must implement policies using nonpartisan discretion. The city council members of a street gang usually represent a political party, therefore it is essential to public administration that when implementing policies that affect the overall community, they do so with nonpartisan intentions and adhere to a utilitarian philosophy. To be successful in politics, a career politician must learn the art of compromise because the decision-making process is one of making choices through a process of conflict, bargaining, and accommodation. (Jillson) In order for the bureaucracy to have a well functioning rule-making process, policy implementation must be based on standards that are applicable to all individuals uniformly. Basically, well-made policies should affect all members of the street gang organization equally and the rules should also produce predictable and certain outcomes on a day-to-day basis without ambiguity. This is not an easy task because policies can often produce imprecise and contradictory goals, and they can be partial to certain groups of individuals. (Jillson)

As was noted in chapter 2, street gang organizations revere evil, while simultaneously maintaining a strong catholic leaning. A very basic policy that most street gang organizations implement is the separation of church and state. In order for the culture of a street gang to be free from religious worship, a secular society must be secured so that religious piety does not get in the way of street warfare. Rousseau once said that, "good Christians make bad citizens," which means that a good Christian is only interested in serving the clergy and will make a bad citizen because he/she will not be interested in serving/ obeying the sovereign state. In street gang organizations, the state has absolute sovereignty and to die for one's state is patriotic and dutiful. If a citizen of the street gang is murdered while demonstrating extreme courage, he dies as a martyr and is remembered as serving the sovereignty of the state with duty and obligation, and was consumed by love of state and glory. During street warfare many citizens are bloodthirsty and intolerant due to the organizational culture of a street gang, thus some breathe murder and slaughter, which becomes a religious experience during the state of war. It is the duty of the city council to refrain from passing policies that interfere with the opinions of the citizens and how they deal with internal ethics and morality because they are constantly engaged in antisocial behavior and street warfare, thus they should not be burdened with a dual obligation with church and state that places them in contradiction with themselves. It is the duty of. the administration to remove those citizens from the social contract that choose not to adhere to the absolute authority of the sovereignty and refuse to sacrifice themselves to their obligation and civil duties. Individuals are constantly encouraged and tested for loyalty, courage, and sacrifice to see if the street gang organization has absolute sovereignty over them and to see how much sovereignty individuals are willing to surrender for the sake of the organization.

According to organizational theory, a prisoner's dilemma exists when there is a conflict of interest between two parties and both parties are trying to maximize their self-interest. The conflict exists when one party acts out of self-interest and their decision adversely affects the other party, therefore they are in a prisoner's dilemma because neither party knows the other's actions. The best solution to the prisoner's dilemma is for both parties to remain quiet, avoid incriminating themselves and the other party, and walk away from the situation unscathed. This is the most significant policy implemented in street gang organizations because the consistent criminal activity and street warfare necessitates the suppression of information. There is an exception to the policy because some information is shared amongst policy makers, members of central committees, some constituents, and other fraternal circles; however, the suppression of information is mostly enforced for personal safety to protect targeted individuals from law enforcement. This policy is statistically significant with domestic assassination and is correlated to capital punishment. Capital punishment is implemented domestically when an individual has snitched on a fellow gang member to receive a lighter sentence or to avoid incarceration and results in the other party receiving a lengthy sentence. It is easy to implement this policy but difficult to enforce because the informant will usually receive protective custody, relocation, and change of identity. The policy can usually be enforced if the informant remains in prison with the general population or if he returns to the same community, and sometimes the informant can receive a pardon by the city council, mayor, and constituents due to general consensus. Capital punishment usually requires paperwork or written documentation providing statements and accusations the informant has made.

Economic policies revolve around fiscal policy and the national tax system. Fiscal policy is the changes in government expenditures and taxes to alter economic variables. Chapter 5 illustrated street gang expenditures and they can increase rapidly due to crisis, conflict, or catastrophe. Healthcare initiatives have usually been unsuccessful because of the heavy tax burden it would impose on individuals. Therefore, healthcare policies are only implemented during a time of crisis when a gang member has been wounded or murdered, and a car wash policy is always implemented immediately to raise funds for the victim and his family. A car wash policy is always implemented in their territory immediately after an individual has been murdered and often times T-shirts and sweatshirts maintaining, "In loving memory of so and so," are worn and circulated, and candlelight vigils are held at the scene of the crime.

Another type of fiscal policy revolves around drug commerce and housing expenditures. During a time of crisis such as a raid or a seizure in which drugs are confiscated from a house/apartment/motel, revenues are expropriated and prevented from circulation; therefore, it is up to the city council members to help make up for lost revenues by providing agricultural subsidies to some members (marijuana/drugs) and relocating drug commerce. After a crisis has transpired, relocation of capital intensive programs is necessary for the maintenance and revenues of the administration, and so working with special interest groups is necessary for the survival and sovereignty of the organization. Many street gang organizations work with special interest groups who engage in drug trafficking and can mobilize product from other countries, although this information is usually not transparent to the general public, and these special interests groups lobby legislators to look out for their best interest. It is common for individuals who are not members of the street gang organization that engage in drug commerce to be burdened with high tariffs for operating within their jurisdiction, however there is usually diplomatic relations with these individuals because the relationship is codependent. The national tax system deals strictly with the tax burden and for every government action there is a public reaction because individuals engaged in capital intensive industries will lobby city council members to reduce their tax burden. Most street gang organizations impose low taxes and provide low services.

Most individual members of street gang organizations are responsible for their own well-being such as food, clothing, medical care, education, employment, and shelter; therefore domestic policies that serve the welfare of the citizenry are limited. The administration provides a low level of services because of the constant state of war and because the organizational culture is individual rather than communal, which means that even though they have a street gang community and practice fraternity and loyalty, it all seems to disappear when they go to jail because that policy is usually, "every man for himself, just don't snitch." Many individuals that go to jail and serve out a prison term feel as though everyone on the outside forgets about them because they rarely get visits or letters, however life on the streets continues and that's just the way the story goes.

Street gang organizations do not provide social welfare programs and individuals are responsible for producing their own capital and are not provided with unemployment benefits, pension plans, or long-term social security. However, the street gang administrations pass policies that contribute to individual's civil liberties such as freedom of speech and association, and civil rights such as anti-discriminatory and minority rights. Freedom of speech is fundamental to the idea of popular government because individuals must be able to participate in public debates and alternatives, and they also have the freedom to associate and petition the existing government. Individual gang members who are dissatisfied with the political climate can associate and petition the existing government, encourage change, and express their concerns without fear of repercussions, however sometimes dissident behavior is considered threatening. Civil rights include anti-discriminatory policies that allow all members of the organization to have equal opportunities and to be able to compete, succeed, and enjoy as does any other member despite race, religion, or gender. Most street gangs are homogenized organizations, yet there are sometimes a small percentage of women, atheists, Satanists, blacks, whites, Asians, and other Hispanics that are not of Mexican descent that make up the demographic, thus their civil rights are protected under these types of policies.

Lastly, because of the constant state of war among street gang organizations, a war policy is implemented amongst neighboring territories to determine behavior towards certain sovereignties. According to nation-states prior to the creation of the United Nations, a declaration of war is the most diplomatic and acceptable policy in regards to a state of hostilities between nations. Any military engagement by a nation must be approved by its legislature, unless it is a clandestine operation, however when in war, there are laws nation-states must adhere to and certain responsibilities must be upheld. For example, neutral nations and civilians must be protected from hostile aggression and violence. However, when laws are ignored by nation-states and crimes against humanity are present in the state of war, they could possibly be charged with war crimes and suffer repercussions amongst the international community. (www.wikipeda.com)   Most wars are about sovereignty, territory, resources, ethnicity, and other issues that are determined later in history, which is also the same for street gang sovereignties. All street gang organizations are engaged in urban warfare, therefore war policy is the most significant and effortless policy to implement and enforce.

Street gang legislatures do not have to approve military engagements because often times a street conflict is random and impetuous decisions must be made by those involved in the conflict. A basic example is when a small group of gang members or a sole individual is driving around, cruising, walking, shopping, partying, or just passing by in a foreign territory, and although they are not looking for a conflict, another group of gang members that control that territory approaches them with hostility and aggression. The standard policy is to "hit them up" or ask them where they are from and if the interrogators are not familiar with the response or the name of their gang, they might respond with aggression by denouncing their gang or simply with physical force. They might respond by asking what regional bloc they are from (in regards to the Los Angeles County) and ask if they have a problem with their neighborhood, or in their terms, "you got shit with so and so!?" Usually if the street gang location is too far, they will give them a pass, allow them as transients as long as they recognize the significant presence of the controlling street gang, and they must make sure to "keep it cool", which means to avoid aggressive behavior. Sometimes, it can result in a battleground as either party can respond with a physical reaction which can result in a street fight, hospitalization, or murder.

As the blood-spattered boulevards shatter the community, a counterattack or a showdown will supercede the previous incident and reinforce the constant state of war. In some situations, the perpetrators will actually go back to the crime scene out of cold-heartedness and curiosity to see how much infliction they have caused, they can report the news to headquarters, thus contributing to their fierce reputation and increasing their war stripes. In some circumstances, they can actually get caught by law enforcement agencies that have a description of the suspects. Street gang organizations have an open policy in regards to witnesses of crime, which can result in open execution or pressure on someone's well-being, thus resulting in a large percentage of deterrence in regards to reporting and identifying criminal activity. This contributes to high-density level communities that digest hideous crimes and become somewhat immune to the street warfare, thus the civilian population must also deal with random violence and sometimes irrational and damaging psychological development. War policy in street gang organizations maintains that civilians should be protected from random shootings and murder, however when there is collateral damage (euphemism for innocent bystanders), the perpetrators can be charged with "crimes against humanity" at the prison congress level and suffer repercussions with their own type of jurisprudence. Based on the hideousness of the crime, it will be assessed on a case-by-case analysis at the local level and the prison congress, resulting in anything from a slap on the wrist to capital punishment.

When dealing with street gang organizations that are not neutral and are considered enemies, the policy is usually to react rapidly and boldly during any run-in or on a mission during a military campaign. In street gang politics, a neutral gang does not mean that the regime does not engage in military combats. A neutral gang refers to a street gang organization that does not conflict in military combats with transients or neighborhoods that are too far to wage a military campaign against. Street gang organizations are in a constant state of war with bordering territories because of the close proximity and the frequent run-ins with each other that lead to small battles, fights, and rumbles that often end in bloodshed. As in any war, the history behind the feud remains biased and ambiguous, therefore a formal declaration was probably never imposed, but the perennial military conflict will continue because of bloodshed. What is important to remember is that when somebody is murdered in street warfare, it is always someone's brother, cousin, uncle, friend, neighbor, etc..., so retaliation will always be expected. Because the enemy is so close, it will render a personal vendetta, sustaining the hostility for years. Because street gang organizations are so spread out and they usurp territory in numerous cities and communities, a state of widespread panic and conflict exists in the Los Angeles County and can be considered a battle zone where combatants engage in constant military campaigns. In traditional war theory, urbanized communities are easier to defend than open spaces because there are plenty of places to hide and wait for enemy activity such as buildings, cars, and trees. Coincidentally, these same factors make it easier for adversaries to creep up and launch a deadly assault unexpectedly using the element of surprise.

Although the social contract is supposed to provide individual gang members with protection from foreign invasion and peace within their jurisdiction, most individual gang members are in a constant state of fear. The fear cannot be transparent because it is destructive in combat, however they all feel it but suppress it because it is contagious and can cause low morale and panic amongst a multitude. Most individual gang members are provincial and stay within their jurisdiction because of the fear of violent death and murder. When traveling for recreational and miscellaneous purposes, they try to stay in territories that do not have a significant gang presence, otherwise they increase their chances of being exposed and fear the suffering of reprisals; they usually want their homeboys to go with them, or they take a weapon to protect themselves. They are constantly looking over their shoulders and actually fear death, yet they act really hard, they have lots of pride, and most will defend their sovereignty with fights and battles that gives them excitement and adrenaline. A simple glance or stare (mad-dogging) can result in aggressive behavior because gang members have a lot of anger and frustration. So if a group/individual is wearing traditional street warfare clothing, if they are staring with hard looks, or if they are driving traditional government vehicles (cars traditionally associated with street gangs such as: Impala's, Regals, Oldsmobile's, Cutlass Supremes, Super sports, and Luxury Sports) they can very quickly become engaged in a showdown that contributes to the cyclical street warfare.

Although urban warfare maintains a clear policy on separation of church and state to avoid a social dichotomy, the duality of man will nevertheless exist due to his psychology vis-à-vis the state of war, which is a perennial phenomenon. Because the state of nature is anarchic, mankind has a natural instinct and inherent violent character that is amplified and becomes an outlet during the state of war. In urban communities that are plagued with street gang organizations, sometimes street warfare is a way to channel the alienation, apathy, disillusionment, and anxiety that is caused by the social dichotomy.

The Mexican American must learn to cope with an identity crisis that internally forces them to be defensive, skeptical, and nationalistic, while simultaneously dealing with outside factors that force them to externally assimilate, embrace, and self-loathe. History has inadvertently taught that the Mexican is illegal, criminal, and antisocial; therefore, this type of behavior is unequivocally expected in the social spectrum, and furnishes a form of self-loathing for many. The self-loathing is displaced and projected against others that look like themselves and those who adhere to the same philosophy, which is the phenomenon of street warfare. They are left with constant frustration while they fight for their soul between good and evil. Some would argue that war is innate and part of the necessary evolution of mankind, however the state of war that exists at the street level is a clear extension of animal instincts such as: territory, competition, and sovereignty, which is reflective of nation-states that have gone to war. The transformation itself is psychologically damaging and irrational to self-development, thus the duality of man is amplified in street gang organizations during a state of war. They are in a constant battle between themselves as they become polarized between positive and negative frictions, thus the rival street gang organization has become the legitimized enemy and they are prevented from seeing the real enemy, which is themselves.

Chapter 7: Congress and County Governments

The California congress is a bicameral legislature with two houses including: an upper house which is the senate, and a lower house which is the state assembly. The Congress meets on a year round basis in Sacramento, which is the state capital, and its legislators are elected from districts and boundaries that are defined by the U.S. census. State senators can serve two terms that last four years, and assemblymen can serve three terms that last six years. The main presiding officers include: a lieutenant governor for the senate, a floor speaker for the state assembly, and the governor who overseas the legislature and who has ultimate executive authority. Most of the work in the legislature is conducted by standing committees, which legislators are assigned to by the speaker, and the Rules Committee appoints all members to all committees, which makes it the governing committee. There are many committees and issues in the state of California because of its size which results in a divided government. Because of the many differences between Northern and Southern California, a significant polarization exists within the legislature. In order for a bill to become a law, it is first introduced by a legislator to the assembly or the senate. It than goes to one or more standing committees for consideration. The committees will then decide which action to take, such as amending it and reporting it to the other chamber for amendment and debate. If accepted without changes, it goes to the governor and if not, it goes back to the original chamber. When it finally reaches the governor it is either accepted or vetoed. (Korey)

According to Bowman, the state legislature has three functions which include: 1.) Policymaking, which is executing laws and distributing funds. 2.) Representation, which includes the constituency from districts and boundaries. 3.) Oversight, which is performance of administration of local/county governments. The state Congress has formal structures; however it also has informal norms and unwritten policies such as emphasizing tenure or superiority of seniority, "paying dues" for rookies, and cue-taking based on partisanship, interest group pressures, arguments and alignment with other legislators, personal agenda or what their conscience dictates, and the behavior of the governor. (Bowman) The state legislature is also responsible for setting up county governments that function as satellite government locations for the state to provide services to residents of certain jurisdictions and boundaries. The counties are made up of boards of supervisors and usually a chief financial officer to assist in the day-to-day activities and administration. The board of supervisors appoints department heads and commission members, yet it also shares executive authority with three independently elected officials including: the Sheriff, District Attorney, and the Assessor. The county is responsible for providing public services such as: social services, healthcare, public protection, public works, regulating land use and development, voting rights, welfare, tax assessment and collection, waste management, and other services through the courts and jails. (Newcomer)

In street gang organizations, the prison system functions as the state Congress with a bicameral legislature with two houses known as the Southside (upper house/senate) and the Northside (lower house/state assembly). The Congress is made up of mostly Southside senators that meet on a year round basis at the state capital, which is the California Institute for Men, located in Chino, California, which is usually known as Chino. The senators and assemblymen who make up the prison system congress are not elected from districts and boundaries, but they are picked up by law enforcement in different districts throughout the state to carry out congressional terms for conducting criminal activities, so they represent districts and boundaries that make up their street gang organization and regional bloc. There are no term limits for prison legislators because some can serve as little as a year, while some can have lifetime tenure and are carrying out a life sentence.

Serving a prison term for conducting criminal activity in a street gang organization does not automatically make someone a Southside senator or a Northside assemblyman. Membership in the Congress depends on street credibility, reputation in the prison system, and political behavior, therefore it is a lengthy process to join the Congress and most of the congressmen are serving out long prison terms. Due to its very nature of secrecy and conspiracy, the prison Congress is a clandestine organization that executes policies amongst the general population, allocates funds to its constituency, represents outside districts and regional blocs (although the Congress has absolute authority), and provides oversight to its county administrations and outside street gang organizations. Most of the legislation done in the prison Congress is also done in standing committees and hearings, however, the Southside senators and Northside assemblymen are completely polarized in the industrial prison complex and a perennial civil war has resulted with sporadic bargaining and negotiating.

The prison Congress is responsible for setting up satellite locations in different prisons in order to enforce policy and implementation; therefore they also have county governments that function as extensions of the Congress throughout the state of California. Currently the state has thirty-two state prisons and fifty-eight county governments, therefore in reference to the prison Congress, there are thirty-one satellite governments which include; Wascow, Avenal, Calipatria, Centinela, Tehachapi, Corona, San Luis Obispo, Norco, Jamestown, Chuckwalla, Tracy, Folsom, Ironwood, Los Angeles County, Ione, Delano, Pelican Bay, Pleasant valley, San Diego, New Folsom, San Quentin, and Susanville, Corcoran, Chowchilla, Vacaville, and Soledad each have two. The county/ satellite prisons are run by a board of supervisors like a county government and a chief financial officer who is the main figurehead or shot caller. However, a county government also has three independently elected officials including: the Sheriff, Assessor, and District Attorney, but in each prison the main shot caller functions as all of those roles. He has complete judicial, legislative, and executive authority over the prison which gives him the power to execute jurisprudence such as crime and punishment, to implement and execute policies, maintain deputies/soldiers, collect taxes, distribute funds, and allocate resources. The shot caller is appointed by the Congress based on political reputation and tenure and usually the position cannot be filled by a rookie because of the informal rule of superiority of seniority. Each prison is run by a chief financial officer (shot caller) with the assistance of a board of supervisors who are responsible for a district, which in prison they consider a yard. There are usually four to five yards per prison, therefore each prison has about four or five supervisors that assist with the day-to-day activities of the prison and appoint department heads to run each building that are labeled from A to E. Moreover, department heads assign staff assistants to run each level in the building, which they call tiers, and usually the complete cycle of assigning public positions is based on patronage which is an informal norm within the prison system.

The industrial prison complex is informally set up as a learning institute for political socialization of the recidivism philosophy. Juvenile Halls are considered elementary schools, California Youth Authorities are high schools, County jails are community colleges, and state prisons are considered universities although some are considered crazier (harder and barbaric) and are referenced as gladiator schools. Ultimately, the prison Congress would be the career criminal/ politician. Street gang organizations on the outside are politically socialized with war theory and engage in consistent battles with adverse street gangs. When entering the jail system for the first time through juvenile hall, an inmate quickly learns to practice tolerance, solidarity, and fraternity with all Hispanic gang members because one of the main policies of prison politics is ethnic identification and solidarity, however there is a small percentage of inmates that represent a different ethnic group rather than their own because the strong affiliation that they have with their street gang transcends ethnic boundaries. Even though inmates and cellmates represent opposing street gang organizations on the outside and they could possibly be in there for murdering one of their comrades, they must practice solidarity as a legislative policy. Occasionally, some inmates will request a personal feud and there are one-on-one fights, however, most usually join the status-quo. Segregation is the most significant policy in the prison system because all formal policies and unwritten norms come from the division of ethnic groups and it is another means of protection within the social contract, which is that all inmates are competing for a scarcity of resources and power. When an individual first enters the industrial prison complex, it's as though he is an immigrant in a war torn battle zone, and he must learn the art of war in order to survive. When a gang member on the outside is engaged in street warfare, it is easier to not get involved because he has an option to renounce membership or stay home and avoid danger, however, when engaged in prison warfare, there are no options because he must consistently engage in warfare and the war is much closer than on the outside. There is nowhere to hide, you cannot stay in your cell, and you will have to "put in work" or suffer repercussions leaving you ostracized and marginalized. Those who decide to renounce their involvement in prison politics and prison warfare end up in protective custody with the worst reputation following them around forever, which leaves them in a constant state of flux and alienation.

Prison policies mandate constant war and segregation amongst Hispanics, whites, and blacks; however the Hispanics are also engaged in a perennial civil war amongst the Southside blue coats/bandanas (Southern California) and the Northside red coats/bandanas (Northern California). The civil war manifests itself in the form of stabbings, murders, and scheduled/random battles that are reflective of medieval battles because it is an all out war using homemade weapons and "anything goes." The riots are usually between the blue coats and the red coats, and between the blue coats and the blacks, and usually the blue coats have more soldiers that will go all the way and fight to the bitter end because they have a lot of heart, discipline, and fear of reprisals from their own, while the red coats and the blacks usually retreat. What results is a divided Congress that practices an intense civil war policy, absolute segregation, consistent feuds amongst different ethnic populations, rendering absolute discipline and solidarity within their ethnic groups. This type of political socialization is reinforced on a daily basis because people are directly influenced by the ecology of their environment. So it is difficult not to succumb to this type of institutionalism, hence the recidivism philosophy.

The recidivism philosophy exists because inmates have become politically socialized in the prison system where certain behaviors, rules, and conduct is the norm, however when they join the real world on the outside they cannot adjust to the rules and norms. They simply continue the criminal behavior that landed them there in the first place because sometimes life is more manageable in prison.

When some inmates are released from prison to join the real world, a sense of schizophrenia exists because they can become completely polarized by an overwhelming world that looks at ex-convicts as substandard humans. Society in general including: family members, employers, law enforcement, friends, neighbors, women they try to court, etc... can contribute to this schizophrenia because society is judgmental and it juxtaposes, and it refuse employment opportunities, thus, the ex-convict feel as though he cannot contribute to society and function as a civil human being.

In prison, categories of good and evil simply cease to control behavior and they do not feel judged by society because they are "out of sight out of mind." When entering the industrial prison complex, inmates must wear a warrior mask and exuberate bravado behavior or be labeled a coward. No matter how old you are, you must consistently prove your courage even though the inner anguish and suffering can become overwhelming. Many feel completely disconnected from humanity. Some do not renounce the moral laws that judged them because they seek out salvation and forgiveness in the form of prayer, and in turn also suffer repercussions from other inmates who look at those who seek out theology as vulnerable and desperate. Most inmates are cognizant that their alienation and consequences are a direct result of their choices, but the sub-standard living conditions of the prison system leave them with a sense of a broken soul and regression.

When first entering the jail system as a teenager, the humiliation and embarrassment of stripping their clothes, the insecurity about their genitals and anatomy, showering with five to ten inmates with small towels, lacking sufficient clothing that fits, using plastic pillows, and the adjusting to unflavored, small portions of food would make anyone recoil and wish they were at home. However, the fear of the unknown becomes routine and inmates learn to adapt to their environment even though they are nostalgic about the outside world and ponder their existence and detachment from a world that was once familiar. The nostalgia becomes suppressed because it makes them vulnerable and they must learn to compartmentalize their depression, live in a bleak existence, and wear a warrior mask with a superhuman cape at all times. Moreover, there is a marginalized group of inmates who suffer much more social stratification, who are the homosexuals, and are manipulated and sometimes coerced into providing domestic, sexual, and financial obligations.

As inmates are released and succumb to the recidivism philosophy, the dark side of the moon seems like a familiar place and the fear of the unknown ceases to exist. When they reenter the prison system they learn to desensitize and mentally prepare themselves for the prison politics and inhumane living conditions that lie ahead. Some make themselves believe that they can have a meaningful existence amongst the prison population because of their knowledge, skills, and abilities within the organizational culture of prison, seeking to become career politicians. Others become disillusioned by the organizational culture and begin to loathe themselves, the prison Congress, and other inmates because of its redundancy and social order.

Chapter 8: The Underground Media

In the United States, the media is protected by the First Amendment of the Constitution that maintains the freedom of the press. The media is supposed to be neutral and independent, and provide the public with information that is necessary, interesting, and essential, and it should be reported without bias. There are many mediums of obtaining public information including: newspapers, magazines, newsletters, television, radio, cable satellite, internet, and word-of-mouth. In today's society, television has replaced the way people procure political information from print newspapers to prime time network news channels. (Abramowitz) Print information such as newspapers and internet sources are mostly used by college-educated individuals, television network channels are mostly viewed by the masses that have a high school education attainment level and lower, and those in the underground countercultures procure information through all mediums of communication, including word-of-mouth and alternative methods.

Print information is more analytical and complex because the reader can interpret the information based on his/her assessment, while television reporting focuses on people's emotional spectrum; it is less complex in delivery and interpretation of ideas, pandering to people's desire for scandal, gossip, and conflict. Furthermore, Marshal McLuhan declares that there are myriads of ways of communicating with the masses, and that those mediums of communication shape their ideas, thoughts, actions, etc... because they subtly alter our perceptual senses, and because the medium itself is the message. He maintains that all technologies are extensions of mankind, and that our central nervous system is super stimulated because of the pseudo environment created around us by different mediums of communication. Some of those other mediums of communication include: speech, dress, infrastructure, artwork, and technology. All mediums of communication help shape people's lives because of the phenomenon and dogma created and associated with different paradigms such as: religious fanaticism, neo-liberal capitalism, or collective racial antagonism. Street gang organizations use many types of mediums of communication to produce a collective militarism that reinforces the socialization of gang behavior, and as a propagandist ideology. In street gang organizations, the medium is definitely the message because they cannot use the popular mediums of communication to get in touch with the masses.

Politicians also use the mass media as a tool to communicate with the general public and their constituencies through expensive spot advertisements and rehearsed speeches. During political campaigns, the mass media covers less information in regards to policy matters, major events, and leadership concerns, and more information on politician's private lives, extramarital affairs, scandal and gossip, and any other type of behavior and information that is sensationalized and interpreted as conflicting and dramatic. As a result, the general public is cynical, unsympathetic, and disillusioned by political journalism because of its lack of essential information, and its abundant reporting on dramatic and incident-based events. Many view the political process as entertainment and sport. They view national elections as horse races, rather than elections, thus resulting in low voter turnout and apolitical behavior. (Abramowitz) According to Stephen J. Wayne, the media is not objective and responsive and is considered to have an ideological and professional bias, but it depends on who interprets the bias. Wayne says that, "Conservative critics often point to studies that show that the majority of national news reporters are Democratic, liberal, and urban-oriented, others point to the influence of conservative corporate executives who oversee the communications empires of radio stations, newspapers, and television networks; to the corporate interests that advertise on these media and contribute to their profits; and to the editorials that reflect the conservative views of the owners, publishers, and advertisers." Wayne also maintains that academic observers perceive a professional bias where the media reports whatever is interesting to most people all the time because it is soft, sensational, and dramatic, and it attracts more viewers, yet it is not accurate and informative; it is not essential to an educated public and electorate. What results is a media that reports incomplete and sensational information that caters to people's emotions, includes ideological polarization of reporting that is either too liberal or too conservative, expresses a professional journalism that is skewed based on reporters' ideas of what is newsworthy, personal ideology, and the amount of audience interest. Nevertheless, it is important to remember that the constitution protects the freedom of the press, which is objective and neutral, and is owned by billion dollar multinational corporations and continuous conglomerate mergers, which dominate the mediums of communication and the airwaves that shift the political culture and ideology of the masses.

Due to the political culture of gangs, street gang organizations use the alternative mediums of communication with a political slant, and informally create a pseudo environment based on propagandist ideology. Gang members in public office also lose their private status and the street media becomes involved with their private lives, extramarital affairs, scandal and gossip, and anything else that is considered dramatic and conflicting. This chapter will examine the mediums of communication that street gang organizations use throughout the street media to alter the perpetual habits of the masses.

In street gang organizations, the media is not used by corporate advertisers to buy consumers, but it is used as propagandist ideology that reinforces the political socialization of gangs, and instead of buying consumers they buy enlistment, fear, and retainment. Street media is conveyed orally through the grapevine and invokes the power of speech and rhetoric to capture audience attention. In the community of Lennox, the radical faction of the far left (Jokers) coined the street media The Lennox Loudspeaker, taken from a monthly newsletter that was published at the Lennox Middle School they attended as children. It is juxtaposed as satire due to its swift travel through the grapevine.

Street gang organizations are always interested in expansion, so they campaign year round through word-of-mouth like tribal and oral cultures to improve enrollment and reduce turnover rates. Their target audience shares the same demographics, thus the public image is considered reflective representation of the constituency, and striking to impressionable adolescents who are considering enrollment. Many gang members use intense grassroots campaigning by seeking support from its residents in the form of persuasion and brainwashing through redundant advertisement. Although they do not use television, radio, and other popular mediums of communication, gang members use spot advertisements on the street to communicate with the general public and their constituencies at local conventions, informal caucuses, public hang outs, and school facilities. Street gang organizations also use wall space like advertisements and political slogans by hitting up the walls with graffiti (usually block letters, wild style, old English, and Roman numerals) that depict their sovereign, to promote against opposing factions and gangs, and using powerful corporate images like the number 13, Surenos, and hand signs to elicit mysticism and reverence. The graffiti itself is an antisocial behavior that allows the content and cryptic messages to be effective communication tools of street media where the medium is the message. Moreover, graffiti style is associated with social class, thus those gang members that usually hit up with abstract style and innovation are considered middle-class, while those that misspell words and lack creativity are considered working-class.

In street gang organizations, class conflict is ostensibly de-emphasized and is not supposed to be a salient theme, however, many street gangs and political parties consider immigration policies and how it will contribute to their public image. Many street gang organizations that do not have a flux of recent immigrants denounce other gangs that have a significant presence of immigrants and insult them with derogatory names such as: wetbacks, dirty gangsters, and chuntaros. Within street gang organizations, factions/political parties are sometimes created around socio-economic status and help contribute to the division of government within their organization. This class conflict that is sensationalized through the mass/street media contributing to factionalism and internal feuding that sometimes exists within street gang organizations. In the late 80's and early 90's, the street organization of Lennox had a problem with class conflict which resulted in fights, riots, and shootings. Although this problem probably exists within most street gang organizations, it is de-emphasized to avoid rendering speculation of division of government to outside observers, and sensationalism throughout the street media.

Speech and dress are also associated with social-economic status, class conflict, and mediums of communication. Many gang members who are second or third generations, have immigrant parents but were raised here in an English-speaking environment, or have mastered the English language, have more confidence in addressing an audience or establishing diplomatic relations. On the other hand, those that speak with an accent, those that have immigrated and have little education in an English-speaking environment, and those that simply cannot or refuse to master the English language, lack confidence and succumb to coyness. They do not usually participate in diplomatic and public relations, they do not normally hold high public office, and they usually join the constituency because of pressure groups and the desire to fit into a strange world.

Furthermore, street gang organizations use backslang that combines English and Spanish, which results in a simple, yet unconventional dialect that uses trickery and smooth talk to alter perception. Marshall McLuhan maintains that, "slang offers immediate index to changing perception that is based on immediate experience and new perpetual habits." What he means is that when backslang is conveyed and exchanged amongst individuals, there is immediate participation amongst them because they have engaged in an altered perception that becomes training for a new habit of conversing. Moreover, when a gang member uses an open platform to address an audience, the entire audience is immediately participating in an altered perception because they are completely involved with trained habit. Once again, the medium is the message because the altered speech itself is an effective communication tool adopted by street gang organizations as an antisocial method that invokes a collective consciousness. Thus, mastering backslang effectively with proper English fluency is positively correlated with socio-economic status, and it can contribute to class conflict.

Although street gang dress code is extremely similar and is meant to be duplicated, the way they wear the clothes, grooming habits, jewelry, and pressing habits, also contribute to socio-economic status, class conflict, and mediums of communication. Gang members that come from a middle-class background wear their clothes with more fashion and finesse than those from the working-class. Middle-class gang members put more thought into their wardrobe such as: constantly keeping up with the latest fashion trends in popular culture, maintaining clean sneakers, pressing their khakis/jeans/shorts to uphold appearances, exhibiting self-sufficient and clean grooming techniques, showing off jewelry that is statistically significant with wealth, demonstrating a variety of articles such as hats, sports jackets, jerseys, sneakers, button-ups, polo shirts, and anything else they wear to show off their surplus wardrobe.

Working-class gang members do not put much thought into their dress code and wear the usual solid colors and conspicuous clothing articles, yet they lack fashion and creativity in regards to style. Class conflict can be physically observed through the act of being clean or maintaining a clean look, which is overemphasized in street gang organizations to substantiate the sovereign's public image. Gang members will constantly praise one another by saying, "Damn fool, you look clean as fuck!" to reinforce socio-economic status as a positive characteristic that is statistically significant with social class and dress. The dress code in general communicates an antisocial behavior as a means to identify themselves with a certain lifestyle, and a way to demonstrate solidarity, uniformity, and equality amongst themselves. It is meant to be conspicuous, and it is a medium of resistance against the consumerist status-quo, the typical rat race, and the standardized behavior of the masses. Street gang organizations cannot meet the demands of the general population and the typical technologies, thus they become non-conformists and seemingly irrational to the homogenized linear thinker. Street gang dress code transforms commonplace perception because it trains people and forces them to associate lifestyle and behavior with dress, consequently communicating a powerful message of propagandist ideology.

Another popular medium of communication throughout street gang organizations and the underground media is urban artwork in the form of drawings, art, lettering, and lyricism. Street art is considered lowbrow due to its uncultivated framework, illegal vandalism, subversive inscriptions, and lack of coloring schemes; however, this type of subversive artwork is not a new phenomenon and is deeply rooted in the ancient civilizations of: Greece, the Roman Empire, Egypt, Turkey, Constantinople, and the Mayans. Many underground countercultures throughout the world have expressed their interpretation of the world through antisocial artwork including graffiti and illegal vandalism on public and private surfaces, thus contemporary street gang organizations have adopted the same ritual. Street gang organizations use public and private surfaces to mark territory and publicly display a significant presence of gang activity, which is challenging to the status-quo and its linear perception. Most urban artwork in street gang organizations is directly influenced by prison life, street struggle and survival, and subconscious surrealism. Engaging in creative artwork is a form of escapism for gang members in prison and on the street, relying on exotic imagery that is revealed through the subconscious mind and exists outside of reason and aesthetic perception, which is characteristic of the surrealist movement. As was mentioned in Chapter 2, street gang organizations and secret societies are notorious for abusing drugs and alcohol to produce ecstasy and enhanced mental states, which allows for creative imagination and perception of street life artistry that reflects: anxiety, apathy, and alienation. Chapter 2 also mentioned commonplace street gang tattoos that serve as iconic propagandist images that can be duplicated by all gang members to demonstrate uniformity and duplication of a collective consciousness. Gang members use their bodies as billboards for political campaigning and promotion for their street gang organization, regional bloc, and the prison senate by tattooing themselves with street gang ideology and imagery that challenges the status-quo.

Those within the artist community of street gang organizations execute their work by tattooing, writing on walls, on letters to and from prisoners, and other miscellaneous items, however most will never have a show at a gallery, or tattoo shop to promote their artistic abilities. In the late 80's and early 90's, two magazines known as Teen Angel and Lowrider Magazine allowed those within the street culture and artist community to submit photographs, paintings, drawings, sculptures, and other such works to be considered for recognition and distinction. Those magazines were used to target a specific audience, which was the street gang culture, and to expedite communication to different regional blocs by merely having a visual impact that sparked curiosity and mysticism. Lowrider Magazine still exists today and has also found a new target audience in Yokohoma, Japan, which results in a cultural exchange because of the presence of the U.S. Navy base there, and has become deeply influenced by the lowrider phenomenon.

Another type of artwork adopted by street gang organizations was the lyrical rhyming influenced by the hip hop/rap community that facilitated communication amongst a multitude through street dialogue that included: backslang rhyming, folk tales, denunciation of rival gangs, and mastery of manipulation, over hardcore instrumental beats. Traditional street gang lyricists would rhyme about war stories, territorial landmarks, love of sovereignty, debauchery, licentious behavior, and excessive denouncement that would compel rival lyricists to contribute their artistic capabilities to the masses. Many lyrical artists in the early 90's came out of the Westside regional bloc of Los Angeles County, and contributed to the underground street raps that dominated the art community and contributed to the propagandist ideology and socialization of street gang organizations. Some of those artists that flourished with popularity and prestige during the early 90's and climaxed during the Renaissance of the Westside (See Chapter 12) included: Youngster and Cartoon from Lennox, Spanto and Jonboy from Culver City, Sneaky from Venice, Spooky from Sawtelle, Boo-Boo from Inglewood, and Tricky from Harpees. The street media would circulate these works to the citizenry of the street gang culture and would later become known as the "Westside Raps" and became extremely coveted by street gang members, the general public, and by the artists themselves.

During the Westside Renaissance, a group of troubadours from the community of Lennox introduced an unconventional style of lyricism that was directly influenced by the Wu-Tang Clan from New York, and NWA (Niggaz with Attitude) from Los Angeles, which resulted in a fusion of conventional hardcore street folk tales, merged with creative style and design that emphasized: impressive vocabulary, highly methodical capabilities, duality of self, and worldwide social concerns. They created their own instrumental beats that were influenced by classical chamber music, gothic/dark wave rock, traditional hardcore/gangster beats, and world music from Latin America, while the lyrical content and style were influenced by beatnik poets, political scientists, civil philosophers, rock 'n' roll musicians, east coast/west coast rappers, religious theology, conspiracy theory authors, anarchist-socialist radicals, and other paradigms and ideologies that help shape world opinions. This group of troubadours was known as The Post Meridians and included members from different political parties/factions that brought different paradigms such as: Puppet and Sporty from the Jokers, D.J. Kraze from the Night-owls, Shadow from the Pee-WeeLocos, and Shy-boy from the Tokers. They also worked with non-government organizations, which in street gang politics are party crews and tagging crews (See Ch.9), and other individuals that had no group affiliations. They were known to have worked with: Sacrifice from Young Wicked Demons (YWD), Sorcery and Scam from Under the Influence (UTI), a producer called Prodigy, and a musician, Pete Chavez, both from the West Side regional bloc. Although they never released any material on a popular or independent label, they did record music at professional recording studios and did promotional work for Julio G. (92.3 The Beat), a demo that was never released, had radio play at a local underground radio station (88.9 KXLU), and their cassettes and CD's still circulate throughout the Lennox underground today.

Urban artwork alters and trains perception like any other art movement, but forces the populace to look at their artwork through a lens of realism and despair, rather than judge it as a consumer commodity or as trained professional art historians or critics.

Infrastructure also has a positive correlation between oral communication and street gang organizations. Information through the grapevine can be facilitated through streets and highways that make it more accessible for those within the street gang culture to travel to new locations. During the early 1990's when the 105 freeway became accessible, gang members from the Westside regional bloc found it easy to travel to areas such as: the Harbor Area, East Los Angeles, Downtown/Central Los Angeles, the Northeast, and South Los Angeles/South Central. Many of those areas had cruising locations, which were sanctuaries for gang activity, such as: Laurel Canyon in San Fernando, Hollywood Blvd in the

Central Los Angeles area, Whittier Blvd in East Los Angeles, and Bristol St in Orange County. These locations provided informal conventions where street gang organizations could roll deep and show their flags, and they could show off their vehicles and significant presence. They could get into battle zones, and they could meet women (hoodrats) from different areas.

One of the main reasons why gang members travel to unknown locations is to meet and party with women from different areas, which is related to their debauchery, and contributes to conflicts of interest with other street gang organizations. When hoodrats party or frequent with gang members, they often invite the gang members to come down to their neighborhoods, despite the fact that it could be a hostile or neutral territory, and allows for those gang members to be caught slipping into darkness (exposed without back-up). The gang member or members who are traveling out of town can find themselves at a party, club, hangout, or any other public place that might allow them to get caught up in a wreck without a hospitable welcome. Hoodrats play a significant role within the street media because they also gossip about scandal, drama, and gang member's public and private lives to friends and relatives, thus news stories begin to circulate within the street community. It is not rare for a gang member from Lennox, to date a girl from Wilmington that he met cruising in Hollywood, and the girl has friends and relatives from a street gang organization that has hostility with Lennox. This hypothetical situation is so common with street gang organizations that many of their feuds revolve around this phenomenon, and it helps contribute to the positive correlation between the grapevine and infrastructure, which facilitates communication amongst the masses. Gang members and people in general, have an overall consensus of pleasure to be around the masses and feel as though they are part of a community or something bigger than themselves. There is a power in numbers that gang members subscribe to, whether it's their own street gang organization, or in community conventions like car shows, cruising spots, or festivals. Marshal Mcluhan maintains that it is a magically subconscious awareness to be around the masses and alter our perpetual senses to this medium of communication. To be part of a collective consciousness is to be part of a global community, regardless if it's a subversive counterculture, and many people do not want to pass up this opportunity or feel as though they are missing out on something bigger than themselves.

Marshal McLuhan professes that the central nervous system becomes super-stimulated in a complex urban social experience, because of the pseudo environment created by different mediums of communication. Individuals in street gang organizations have a super-stimulated central nervous system because of the complex state of war in their neighborhoods, and because of the different mediums of communication that reinforce the propagandist ideology of the street gang culture. The central nervous system becomes desensitized to the complex violence experienced in street gangs, and it learns to effectively cope and compartmentalize actions and reactions. The central nervous system commands all physical activities, while stimulating mental consciousness; therefore it becomes super-stimulated because the social experiences in the street gang culture are overwhelming. When the central nervous system becomes exposed to this type of stimulation, it must succumb to numbness or it will result in extreme polarization of the mind. The social order and structure of street gang organizations forces gang members to numb themselves to the policies and procedures of the organizational culture, and adopt the violent behavior that comes with the social contract. When joining the social contract, the central nervous system must decolonize itself from practical actions/reactions, and learn a complex method of responding to stimuli. Outside observers and the citizenry living within street gang organizations also become infected through the central nervous system because they must also respond differently to the policies and procedures adopted by street gang organizations. Because they live in a constant atmosphere of gang activity, they must also succumb to numbness and respond to stimuli in a different way.

The general public responds differently to violent crimes that are witnessed because of the jurisprudence that street gang organizations enforce, and because the well-being of non-gang members is not protected in street gang territories. The street media attacks the central nervous system through all mediums of communication, including technology, because it forces people to respond differently to the super-stimulation in their complex pseudo environment. Marshal Mcluhan says that all technologies are extensions of ourselves, which makes us become stimulated by them, therefore we embrace technologies through a narcissistic fashion. We embrace our technologies, they are extensions of ourselves, and we serve some objects/technologies because they become natural to our existence. Some of these objects become extensions of us and it seems as though they cannot be separated because they are one and the same with mankind. Men have always had a sexual relationship to the motorcar and people in general talk about having dream cars, and street gang members are no different so they also have a sexual relationship to the motorcar. As was mentioned in Ch.6, there are certain vehicles that are associated with street gang culture, and because this is an assessment of the political culture of gangs, those motorcars become government vehicles. Gang members become obsessed with certain vehicles and have them look a certain way to convey the propagandist ideology. For example: Cutlass Supreme or Buick Regal with European front end, Luxury and Super Sport Monte Carlo, El Camino, Chevrolet Impala, Cadillac, etc...and others, which usually range anywhere from the 1960's to the present and sometimes include whitewalls, lowered with rims, sound system, or stock. The vehicle becomes an extension of the driver and turns him into a superhuman, which allows him to invoke an image similar to the knight with horse and armor. Owning these types of vehicles give the driver super status and empowerment that allows these individuals to serve this object of technology with great reverence. Government vehicles are coveted by gang members because they help reinforce the street gang culture by being tools of communication through standardization and repeatability.

Another technology that is an extension of mankind and is an object of obsession for the gang member is the gun and shank (knife). Street gang organizations are in a constant state of war, so weaponry is also an important object of technology. The philosophy of street gang organizations is to "live and die by the gun/sword," so it is commonplace for gang members to get tattoos of weaponry on their bodies. Weaponry plays a strong and significant role in street gang organizations because individuals serve those objects with great reverence. It gives them superhuman powers that other technologies are incapable of. Many individual gang members even feel naked without their vehicle and weapon and feel as if they cannot function with their missing technologies. For street gang organizations, these technologies are extensions of them, they are mediums of communication, and they reinforce the propagandist ideology.

When individuals from street gang organizations come up to the surface from the underground, anywhere above sea level, they discover that the popular media demonizes their culture, but simultaneously promotes their mysticism and awe. Coincidentally, the United States citizenry has always had an obsession with gang culture since their fascination with bootleg gangsters from the 20's, to the contemporary interpretation of street gang culture today. Popular mediums of communication such as: television shows, movies, network news channels, radio, internet, newspapers, and books have all contributed to the romanticism and glorification of gang culture. During the early 1990's, Fox 11 news had a reporter (Chris Blatchford) who investigated the phenomenon of street gang organizations and would have news specials that assessed the dramatic conflict of street gang culture. Chris Blatchford specialized in sound bites designed to capture public attention. He had his target audience glued to the television to stay tuned for exhilarating war stories and information in general about street gang politics. Chris Blatchford always had live footage that was raw and "in your face" that exposed counterculture activity, and would cater to people's emotional spectrum by taking their lifestyle and putting it under a magnifying glass. Those who participate in counterculture activity, those who live in gang-infested communities, those who have family members in that kind of lifestyle, and anyone who has become socialized to their existence has a sympathetic and scornful dual approach to street gang organizations. Watching news specials about prison riots, urban warfare, and individual lives of those in street gang organizations, helps gang members appear humane and emotional, but they are conflicted by the social contract they have joined. Chris Blatchford's voice catered to people's sensitivity by stimulating their senses visually by demonstrating gang member's hard exterior surface, then following a storyline that involves conflict and scandal with a subtle plea for understanding and compassion.

Another popular medium of communication that romanticizes gang culture is the film industry. Films such as: Boulevard Nights, American Me, Colors, Blood in Blood Out, and Training Day, also contribute to the glorification/demonization of street gang culture by taking their lifestyle and putting it up on the big screen and catering to an international audience. Gangster films have always done really well domestically and internationally. Some of the fictional/non-fictional superhuman characters depicted in those movies have generated an obsession with their personalities such as: Scarface, The Godfather, Keyser Soze from "The Usual Suspects", Al Capone, and John Gotti. Gangster films appeal to those engaged in counterculture activity because it validates their subversive lifestyle, and they glorify crime to the extent that it gives them false hope of believing they can live a life of fast cash, loose women, and material possessions, while rendering prestige and respect amongst their peers. Gangster films have directly influenced many individuals in the hip hop community that adopt gangster pseudonyms, lifestyles, style of dress, and merge it with their own microcosmic urban struggle using it in their songs, videos, and films. Rap artists have taken the streets to the stage and sell their urban lifestyle, struggle, and hustle, to mainstream multicultural America, and to international communities that imitate the lifestyle they live and die for. Rap moguls Eazy E, Tupac Shakur, Biggie Smalls, and Duke (Psycho Realm) have all suffered fatalities that were caused by their street life philosophy. In the early 90's, a bicoastal feud began between west/east coast gangster rappers that revolved around contravene verses, women, differences in lifestyle, dress, and other mediums of communication adopted by the differences between Los Angeles and New York. The bicoastal feud resulted in stabbings, shootings, jail sentences, and murders, which were triggered by overt hostile aggression, and the sensationalized drama that the popular media exploited because of the conflict, gossip, and scandal. Other popular mediums of communication that glorify/ demonize street gang/prison culture include: The Homies toy line depicting gang members and the street culture, internet websites like www.streetgangs.com, popular clothing brands that embrace counterculture activity, television commercials that use elements of gang culture, video games that depict street gang organizations and urban lifestyles, and popular television shows such as "The Sopranos" and "Oz" that explore gangster culture with an empathetic perspective. (See Epilogue)

The popular media is partially responsible for its love/hate relationship between street gang organizations and the masses by sensationalizing events and embracing certain gang figures as having lots of charisma and prestige, which leads to the dubious association between gangs and the citizenry. The majority of the population is interested in journalism and mediums of communication that revolve around scandal, gossip, and conflict, therefore any news reporting that investigates street gang organizations is embraced because it contains those elements. Popular mediums of communication should provide information that is essential, interesting, and necessary, but because the market dictates the outcome of news stories, it provides the citizenry with scandal, gossip, and conflict that helps create a pseudo environment that over stimulates our central nervous system. What results is the contribution of the popular/street media to the dumbing down of society, and the decadence of modern culture by attacking the central nervous system and mutating actions/reactions because of gang politics, and helping reinforce the propagandist ideology of street gang organizations.

Chapter 9: Interest Groups

All interests groups seek to influence government decision-making by pressuring legislators to pass policies that are beneficial to them. Most interest groups are non-government organizations or independent associations with common interests, and many are non-profit organizations that have the public and the consumer's interests in mind. Usually, interest groups are social/cultural groups, whose primary goal is not commercial, they maintain a consultative status with government organizations, and they use lobbying as their primary technique to influence government decision-makers. In order to influence legislators, lobbyists need access and connections, which usually includes an informal "wine and dine" session, or simply establishing rapport and friendships with legislators to help influence decisions based on loyalty and empathy.

In the subterranean street culture, there are interest groups that lobby street gang legislators to pass policies on their behalf such as: party crews, tagging crews, non-profits, drug lords, and law enforcement. Party crews are social groups whose primary concern is debauchery, partying, fraternity, and they seek to influence street gang legislators because they often loiter in gang-infested territory and sometimes seek access to government conventions and festivals. Tagging crews are social groups whose primary concern is urban artwork and graffiti, and they seek to influence street legislators because they compete for wall space, which sometimes results in serious repercussions for tagging crews. Non-profit organizations include: Homies United and Victory Outreach, whose primary concern is to rehabilitate individual gang members and help them escape urban/prison politics and resume a civilian lifestyle. Drug lords are independent of gang politics, but engage in commerce in inner cities and lobby street legislators for sovereignty and customers. Lastly, law enforcement agencies are special interest groups because they play a significant role in the prevention and eradication of street gang organizations, "by all means necessary," and sometimes resulting in corruption and scandal. Law enforcement agencies seek to influence street legislators through intimidation and prevention; however coercion and blackmail are often lobbying techniques employed.

In the Westside regional bloc of Los Angeles County, many party crews developed in the early 90's to maintain fraternity, prestige, and reputation amongst their peers, but avoided joining a social contract because of the violence and pressure of street gang organizations. Some of these party crews included: Mexican Power, Tres Equis, Insane Rascals, Woodtown Posse, 2 Skanless, 100% Players, Kick Nuts, Super Crew, and Crazy Sex, which were usually associated with a certain street gang organization because of their geographical location. Party crews originated as groups of like-minded individuals and friends who had a common interest in partying as their main objective, and protection for themselves from street gang organizations and other party crews/cliques. Sometimes they adopted pseudonyms, they emphasized a clean look with expensive clothing and style, they drove nice vehicles, and they maintained popularity and reputation amongst the ladies. Party crews feuded with each other because of territory, women, reputation, and association, which are similar to street gang organizations, and other groups of individuals, and occasionally engaged in more violent activity. Because of their geographical location, party crews were usually associated with the street gang organization in their territorial stomping ground, for example: Mexican Power, Tres Equis, and Insane Rascals, were associated with Lennox 13 because of their resident status in Hawthorne and Lennox. Woodtown Posse and 2 Skanless were associated with Inglewood 13, 100% Players were associated with Hawthorne Piru Gang, Super Crew was associated with Culver City 13, and Crazy Sex was associated with Santa Monica 13. As party crews increased in size and reputation, street gang organizations began to perceive them as potential members with promising careers, and began putting pressure on these associations.

Party crew members began lobbying efforts to prevent street gang organizations from passing policies that targeted their members as enemies. Street gang organizations rely on fear and intimidation and often view party crews as weak associations, thus they sometimes impose intimidation practices and pressure them to join the street gang organization. Some party crew members maintained close relations with decision-makers, established connections with influential gang members, and played a consultative role to legislators that had the authority to allow them sovereignty without fear of intimidation and repercussions, and avoiding a coercive draft. However, lobbying techniques were not always successful and sometimes lasted shortly, for example: Mexican Power became extremely politicized, maintained sovereignty for a few years, and were later drafted into Lennox, and became a political party/clique. Tres Equis were drafted into Lennox and mostly joined the Jokers clique, and Woodtown Posse was drafted into Inglewood Rascals. Furthermore, during the Westside Renaissance, many party crews were extremely generous with their lobbying techniques because of the prestige and reputation of the festivals and conventions of the time period, thus seeking access to those cultural events. (See Ch.12) When party crew members get drafted into a street gang organization, they usually bring their socialization of the party crew association with them and inadvertently help transform the overall ideology of the organizational culture of their political party or street gang, and thus become agents of change. Party crews were originally meant to party and establish fraternity, however they sometimes had conflicts with street gang organizations and begin feuding, so they joined a gang or merged within the gang, and the conflicts of interest they had with other party crew associations led them to violent behavior that was typical of street gang culture. Therefore, party crews were sometimes considered interest groups because of their association and involvement with street gang organizations, and their lobbying techniques used to influence decision-makers.

In the late 80's and early 90's, the tagging/graffiti phenomenon took the Los Angeles County by storm. Most individual graffiti writers/artists were associated with a crew, and tagging crews were emerging from thin air and dominating the street subculture, which was threatening street gang organizations. The main objective of a graffiti writer was to gain street recognition by defacing public/private property continuously, and joining a crew that had a notorious reputation. Graffiti writers were known for tagging their individual aliases and crews on any kind of infrastructure, they would bomb buses, and they would consistently engage in battles with other tagging crews. It was commonplace activity for graffiti writers from opposite crews to hang around bus stops and take turns bombing a bus to see who was the most daring, who had the most style, and who had the most members willing to risk their freedom for the sake of the battle and the association. Tagging crews were social groups with a common interest of street recognition and urban artwork and their primary goal was not commerce, however, their subculture activity often conflicted with street gang organizations, and they became special interest groups that aimed for a utilitarian framework for their members. Many gang members were known to intimidate and punk graffiti writers because of their subordinate status with street gang organizations, however many tagging crews and specific individuals within that community had fierce reputations and were competing for honor and bravery, thus becoming forces not to be reckoned with.

Graffiti writers and tagging crews already had a subversive stigma because of their lack of respect for private/public property, but they had other criminal elements attached to them such as: racking (stealing), experimenting with and selling drugs, carrying illegal firearms, and occasionally engaging in physical violence against opposite crews. This resulted in certain graffiti writers and tagging crews becoming politicized by the street gang philosophy and started behaving more like gang members. Some began dressing and writing like gang bangers, some actually joined a gang and had a dual sovereignty to the street gang organization and their tagging crew association, and some merged their tagging crew within a street gang or became an actual street gang organization. Some of these tagging crews included: KWS, which originally stood for Kings with Style, later to be known as Krazy Wicked Surenos, and also a political party/clique to 18th St. NBT, which stood for Nothing but Trouble became Trouble Gang, and many of their associates joined black street gang organizations as Bloods and Crips. (It should be noted that a crucial distinct element that differentiates street gang philosophy from tagging crew philosophy is that most tagging crews are multicultural groups that champion diversity, while street gang organizations keep their diversity to a minimum). KAK, which stood for Known as Kings, became part of Compton Barrio 70's (CV70's), FSK, which stood for Fuck Society Crew mostly joined Lennox 13 and Lawndale 13, NTS, which stood for Next 2 Serve joined the Florencia 13 gang, and ATC-Addicted to Crime, KMT-Krazy Mexican Taggers, TMC-The Magician's Club, all became their own street gang organization. During all the hoopla of tagging crew sovereignty and graffiti writers becoming politicized, this in turn coined the term "tag bangers"; there were a lot of lobbying efforts on behalf of tagging crew associations with street gang organizations. Individual graffiti writers and tagging crews would lobby street gang legislators to allow for their sovereignty, to protect them against other street gangs or opposing tagging crews, and provide illegal firearms and drugs. These lobbying techniques were usually successful for a variety of reasons, however, a county-wide policy implemented during the Treaty of the South Side from 1993-1994 by the Prison Congress (See Ch.11) imposed a green light on tagging crews and enforced a draft, which reversed lobbying techniques that had previously been successful. Not all tagging crews were affected by this policy, yet many joined the street gang organizations and an increase in gang membership was statistically significant. Similar to party crews, tag bangers that joined a street gang brought their tagging crew socialization with them and helped transform the overall ideology of street gang organizations, and played a significant role as change agents during the Westside Renaissance.

Drug dealers operate and coexist with street gang organizations in the inner cities; however, they also operate in middle class suburbs and sell drugs to the more affluent users. The difference between the suburban drug dealer and the inner city dealer is that those in the inner city must succumb to taxation without representation. Many drug dealers operating in the inner cities share the same customer base with street gang organizations, and also have street gang members as part of that commerce. Often times, those drug dealers have serious connections throughout other states and countries, and gang members need access to their availability of resources to keep their administration afloat. Drug dealers are a special interest group, whose primary objective is commerce. They transcend state and international borders and they use lobbying techniques when dealing with street gang organizations.

Many drug dealers involve their entire families in the operation including: brothers, sisters, parents, aunts, uncles, children, and so forth, so a main concern for them is overall protection and well-being. Because there is a fear of intimidation and fear of getting jacked by street hoodlums, they lobby street gang legislators for protection and sovereignty. Many drug dealers are allowed sovereignty; however they do have to pay taxes on their revenues and do business with the street gang organization within those boundaries. Lobbying techniques on behalf of drug dealers are ambiguous because they sometimes obtain protection and sovereignty, but they sometimes get jacked, threatened, and physically harmed by gang members. Drug dealers lobby urban politicians to pass policies that are beneficial to them and contribute monies to their campaigns to procure adequate representation. The relationship between the drug dealers and street gang organizations is one of necessity and reciprocity because they both need each other for survival; however, street gang legislators make secret deals with drug dealers behind closed doors and avoid accountability and transparency to the general public and their constituencies.

Non-profit organizations including; Homies United and Victory Outreach, are non-government organizations that help victims and victimizers of street gang violence escape a life of criminal propagandist ideology. Victory Outreach is a community-based church organization that helps lost and troubled souls find their way to Christ, specifically in the inner cities. Although it is a highly recognized international organization, it has a very significant presence around the Los Angeles County because of its successful effort in the rehabilitation of street gang members. Since the 60's, it has played the role of a special interest group to street gang organizations because of its lobbying efforts to end street gang violence. Because of the separation of church and state in street gang organizations, it does not have as much overall influence on the organizations; however, individuals are drawn in on a personal level that has more sovereignty than their commonwealth. Victory Outreach throughout the Los Angeles County involves the arts including: music, poetry, literature, film, and playwriting, to capture an audience that has been socialized by street gang philosophy and sees the dramatization of it in the arts as a way to elude it. Many high-ranking officials from the Prison Congress, and also street-level urban politicians have renounced their involvement in street gang/prison politics and have given their lives to Christ as a path to salvation, forgiveness, and repentance. Victory Outreach helps to facilitate the transition from street gang hoodlum to law-abiding citizen, and lobbies street gang politicians to not seek personal vendettas on those who have found a higher meaning in life, but encourages more soldiers to go on missions for Christ, specifically here in the City of Lost Angels.

In 1996, a non-government outreach organization in El Salvador began the process of dealing with an overwhelming gang epidemic that had plagued the nation. Throughout the 90's, the United States began dealing with an overcrowded prison population, and saw the deportation of illegal immigrants as an alternative solution. Most of those illegal immigrants were also criminals who were engaged in street gang organizations in Los Angeles County, but were born in Mexico, Honduras, Guatemala, Nicaragua, and El Salvador. Coincidentally, when these illegal criminals were imprisoned for street gang activity, they were also deported to their countries of origin, even though they had been completely socialized in the United States. This led to the widespread activity of street gangs in the Central American region and its proliferation. Homies United began as a proactive organization to deal with this epidemic that had swept through the region, specifically with the notorious MS, which is the Mara Salvatrucha. MS is known as a ruthless street organization that has is roots in

Los Angeles, and began exporting its code of honor and existence throughout Central America and various major cities throughout the United States, which was directly caused by the deportation of illegal criminals. (See Ch. 10)

Homies United was an organization created by ex-gang members to deal with street gang defectors that no longer want to uphold the social contract, but need protection because they fear repercussions from their former street gang organization. Homies United opened a Los Angeles chapter two years after its origin in El Salvador, and has since lobbied street gang politicians to eradicate gang violence, to allow defectors to walk away peacefully without reprisals, and to join grassroots struggles in political activism against police brutality, misconduct, and racism. During the Rampart Scandal of the LAPD, Homies United and other street gang members were involved in the National Day of Protest to Stop Police Brutality, and found themselves aligned with other political activists. Many of those gang banger activists marched to the LAPD headquarters and protested against police brutality, which many gang members have direct connections with, and were extremely open with accusations. Because of their exposure of police brutality, racism, and misconduct, LAPD officer's targeted Homies United officials and other gang members within the area, however, it wasn't long before the LAPD's Rampart Scandal attracted international attention, and was involved in federal civil rights lawsuits and corruption scandals. Most gang members perceive police officers as gangsters with badges because their conduct towards street gang organizations goes beyond the law and often involves corruption, misconduct, coercion, and blackmail. Sometimes police officers are also considered special interest groups because they also use lobbying techniques when dealing with street gang organizations including; prevention, commerce, and corruption. In 2002, the LA Weekly published an article that outlined the history of LAPD scandals which included: 1902-1905, corruption scandals force 5 LAPD police chiefs to retire. 1922-1923, more than 100 police officers discharged for police brutality. 1926- LAPD declares war against organized crime and bootleg gangsters; philosophy is "wanted dead or alive." 1936- Following the invasion of depression refugees, police chief usurps state power and imposes a "bum blockade" against migrant workers. 1943- Sailors from Chavez Ravine Navel Base riot against Mexican-American teenagers and LAPD arrests victims, which is than followed by Zoot Suit riots. 1951-Event known as Bloody Christmas because of the bloody brutality 7 Latinos received while in police custody. 1965- Watts riots sparked by controversial arrests. 1975- 1982, 15 people die from being subdued by notorious police chokeholds. 1982- LAPD increases anti-gang units after black gang members begin to proliferate. 1988- Mass gang sweeps throughout Los Angeles county including Hispanic/black gang members who are given jail time for practically anything. 1992- Race riots followed by Rodney King beating and acquittal of 4 police officers. 1998- Rampart scandal, where CRASH officer, Rafael Perez, is arrested for stealing 6 pounds of cocaine and implicates 70 officers in police corruption and misconduct. (Joe Domanick)

The 1992 Los Angeles race riots were triggered by judicial injustice and police brutality. After 1 Hispanic and 3 white police officers were acquitted by an all white jury for beating an unarmed incoherent motorist, which was videotaped by an objective onlooker, disillusioned inner city proletariats began rioting in the streets of Los Angeles. Racial profiling and police brutality had reached a climax, thus the verdict of the trial sparked a collective opportunity for mostly low-income blacks/Hispanics to engage in mass law-breaking including looting, arson, and random shootings. Within hours, the streets of South Central Los Angeles turned into a battle zone as proletariat looters and snipers shot at police officers, rescue workers, media/police helicopters, and Korean shopkeepers with assault weapons they had looted from surplus stores. Multiracial rioters used Molotov cocktails to torch motorcars, block intersections, and systematically burned capitalist enterprises and government buildings, which forced law enforcement agencies to withdraw from the battle zone. Mass looting and rioting spread to other locations including Lennox, which forced state officials to declare a curfew, send in federal military troops and set up a barracks at the Lennox Sheriff station and other focal points of interest or targets for rioters, which were in the middle of urban neighborhoods. Many viewed the Los Angeles riots as opportunist anarchy used for personal benefit because many luxury goods had been looted, however, it was a period of social unrest where proletariats joined forces and focused on the common enemy, which included law enforcement, the market economy, and the bourgeoisie.

Many street gang organizations were heavily involved in the 1992 Los Angeles riots, however, many of them used it as an opportunity to settle scores with hostile states and police officers. Those individuals that make up the proletarian underground counterculture, had enough collective influence and disillusionment to bring the city of Los Angeles to a standstill, and helped trigger collective spontaneous rioting in other cities including: San Francisco, San Jose, Las Vegas, Tampa, Seattle, Atlanta, New York City, Oakland, Chicago, Phoenix, Madison, and Berlin. (www.libcom.org/history)

In 1998, CRASH officer; Rafael Perez was arrested for stealing 6 pounds of cocaine from an LAPD evidence room. CRASH (Community Resources against Street Hoodlums) was an elite anti-gang unit created by the LAPD to suppress gang activity and gather intelligence on street gang organizations. In order to infiltrate street gang organizations, CRASH officers had to know everything about street gangs for example; history, origin, who are the shot callers, pseudonyms, girlfriend's/ moms houses, what cars they drove, what tattoos they have, and any other intelligence that can be of possible use to them. In many ways, those police officers had to socialize with gang members, understand the neighborhood mentality, and adopt their thought process to anticipate the subsequent moves of gang members. This is what led the CRASH units to have a stigma attached to them as a police gang, specifically in the Rampart Division because they had "their own way of doing things," which was cutting corners, being unsupervised, and exercising their own jurisprudence. CRASH officers had a logo, plaques, matching tattoos, patches on jackets, and were also rewarded and recognized for having hits and killings, similar to gang members, having stripes for shootings and murders. After Rafael Perez was arrested, he exposed and implicated at least 70 other police officers in patterns of misconduct including; brutal beatings, bad shootings, routine lying, writing false reports, planting drugs and guns on gang members, and selling street drugs. This was known as the Rampart Scandal, and was also associated with the arrest of police officer David Mack for a bank robbery, who was a good friend of Rafael Perez, and who was a possible suspect in the killing of rapper Biggie Smalls. David Mack and Rafael Perez had been known to work security for the Death Row record label, which had strong ties with a blood gang from Compton, and were also seen in numerous pictures throwing up blood hand signs and dressed all in red. (www.streetgangs.com) CRASH officers in Culver City were also known for their pattern of misconduct, and in 1994 the unit received a blow to its public image for locking up two Culver City 13 gang members in a holding tank with rival enemies, Venice Shoreline Crips, which were subsequently beaten for hours without police intervention. In the unincorporated community of Lennox, the Lennox Sheriff were also engaged in patterns of misconduct including: a regional injunction that was later challenged by civil rights organizations, routine beatings for disobedience and lack of cooperation, dropping off gang members in rival neighborhoods to see fights or just so they can get caught slipping, drinking on the job, confiscating drugs/monies/weapons without arresting perpetrators, drive-by macing, implementing physical damage to motorcars, locking car keys inside of gang member's motorcar trunk, and blackmail.

Throughout the Los Angeles County, police officers that patrol gang territories are known for their misconduct and jurisprudence which most street gang organizations can relate to. The events in Rampart, Lennox, and Culver City, are precedent examples that question the legitimacy of street patrol units that abuse their authority and violate civil rights. Corrupt police officers are sometimes responsible for long prison terms because many individuals do not have enough resources to protect themselves from the judicial system that offers them plea bargains versus life sentences. All street gang organizations consider law enforcement agencies real and natural enemies, thus police officers have often been targets of violence because of their conduct towards those in the subculture. When police officers are gunned down in the line of duty, police officers retaliate with a personal vendetta and come down hard on the street gang organization that has assumed responsibility for the murder, and start arresting and booking suspects for crimes that result in harsh prison sentences. In May of 1993, an off-duty police officer from the Hawthorne Police Department murdered the most popular representative of the Lennox Mexican Power clique, which resulted in retaliation against the department, and left a few individuals incarcerated for long prison terms. Law enforcement units that patrol street gang territories are special interest groups that undermine the sovereignty of street gang organizations "by all means necessary," and become perennial enemies to street gang organizations and others belonging to the counterculture.

Chapter 10: International Relations

After nation-states have exploited their domestic resources and a battle for scarcity, power, and wealth develops, they begin to move beyond their territory to accumulate land, capital, and labor. The struggle for regional power means that nation-states must make preparations for defense and build up their military capabilities to extend their sphere of influence throughout the region. Through the use of force, intimidation, and propaganda skills, nation-states strive for power, national security, and domination, thus usually resulting in a regional hegemony, where one state has influence over other states' foreign/domestic affairs. The regional hegemon uses its military capabilities to influence the international community and begins annexing resources and/or land, setting up commonwealths and colonies, engaging in foreign direct investment to increase their gross national product (GNP), and finding innovative ways to influence states to pass policies that are beneficial to them. Social contracts were created because the state of nature is anarchic and a balance of power is necessary, however in the international community, the atmosphere is much more anarchic and pronounced because it is a macrocosmic perception, and nation-states do not want to be dominated by a regional hegemon that tries to undermine their sovereignty. During the middle of the 20th century, the international community started moving into a global village where information and technology became more important for wealth and domination rather than land and labor, therefore creating virtual states that are more cost-efficient and can produce goods and services overseas and sell them on the foreign market. Virtual states invest in human resources, technology, and information, and compete for power and national security on the international stage; therefore, the new struggle for power does not necessarily involve armed conflict.

The world is divided between three different ideologies of international political economy, including Marxism, liberalism, and mercantilism/nationalism. Liberalism maintains that politics and economics are two separate spheres of influence that are not dependent on each other and that economic policy should be dictated by the free market. In order to maximize efficiency, establish economic thrift, and maintain individual welfare, a market economy develops spontaneously based on the principles of supply and demand. Individuals create and facilitate markets for trade and exchange to satisfy consumer needs, and naturally increase the range of goods and services so that both parties in the exchange benefit, trading goods and services voluntarily. The basic concept of liberalism and the market economy is to improve their well-being in the scheme of things, therefore rationalizing a cost/benefit analysis in regards to goods and services and maintaining economic growth. Mercantilism/nationalism maintains that economic growth and activity are subordinate to the objective or goals of the nation-state, which can range anywhere from having a peaceful, neutral state without a military, to a totalitarian fascist regime. Mercantilists believe that the sovereignty of the state is dependent on the wealth of the nation and its power, therefore economic resources and policies are necessary for national security and development. Economic and political decisions are made simultaneously because they are dependent on each other for the same goal of wealth and power; however, the interests of the nation-state are primary. Jacob Viner maintains that, "1. Wealth is an absolutely essential means to power, whether for security or for aggression; 2. Power is essential or valuable as a means to the acquisition or retention of wealth; 3. Wealth and power are each proper ultimate ends of national policy; 4. There is long-run harmony between these ends, although in particular circumstances it may be necessary for a time to make economic sacrifices in the interests of military security and therefore also of long-run prosperity." In regards to the international community, mercantilists believe that self-sufficiency is necessary for wealth and power even though the benefits are disproportionate to other nation-states. Marxism developed as a reaction to capitalism and the market economy because the means of production that are privately owned exploit wage labor, thus transforming labor into a dispossessed commodity that can be traded and exchanged as goods and services. Marxism criticizes capitalism and maintains that its demise is inevitable because of three economic laws which are: disproportionality, which is that capitalism, tends to overproduce products, goods, and services that consumers cannot afford and causes periods of instability in the market economy. Secondly, that capitalism is governed by fierce competition and profit that forces the accumulation of wealth in the hands of the bourgeoisie (middle-class), and forces the exploitation of the working class proletariats. Lastly, that the falling rate of profit, which decreases the incentive to invest, save, and accumulate, increases unemployment levels and leads to economic stagnation and poverty. Marxism believes that the impoverished proletariat will rise up and overthrow the bourgeoisie with a social revolution and replace the economic system with a socialist agenda. (Charles W. Kegley, Jr.)

In the late 80's, the street gang organization of Lennox began its efforts at expansion with a move to the Downtown/ Central Los Angeles regional bloc of the Los Angeles County in the Hollywood area. Street gang areas usually have a high-density level that makes the market economy and commerce a bit saturated, so some individuals from Lennox began relocating to the Hollywood area to extend their sphere of influence and to exploit available resources. Often times, individual gang members are in hiding and running from law enforcement agencies, so they end up in open and sometimes hostile territories and take their lifestyle with them. The Lennox 13 gang started a commonwealth in the Northeast regional bloc called the Hollywood Bandits and began recruiting impressionable youths and known comrades, expanding their network of trade, colonialism, and influence. As a small colony with a fatherland in a different regional bloc, the Hollywood Bandits had to deal with open hostility from other established gangs within the area including: 18th St, Mara Salvatrucha, Armenian Power, The Magician's Cub, and other well-known street gang organizations within the region. With assistance and resources from Lennox headquarters, the Hollywood Bandits were able to establish a tight-knit commonwealth that engaged in racketeering, extortion, murder, and drug commerce, however, because of their illegal activities and pressure from law enforcement, they would relocate like wandering vagabonds to North Hollywood, Eagle Rock,

Highland Park, and Anaheim. In general, many gang members are forced into exile by law enforcement because they are wanted for criminal activities, and they relocate to areas where family, friends, relatives, or other networks are in place, thus they take their lifestyle with them and reinforce the propagandist ideology of Los Angeles street gang culture.

Many South Siders, which includes any gang member from a Southern California gang, migrated to Las Vegas, Nevada in the early 90's because it was wide open for drug trafficking and street gang organizations were not in place. Many Lennox boys migrated to Las Vegas because of forced exile, labor, and other reasons, and established networks with other South Siders, to help expand the propagandist ideology of gang culture. The struggle for power and wealth develops in any area where market economies develop to provide an availability of resources based on the principles of supply and demand, especially when the protagonists establish a mercantilist agenda. In Las Vegas, local residents developed their own street gang organizations to resist the outside influence that the South Siders brought with them; therefore, the South Siders established networks and loose coalitions to build up their defense and national security.

Many Lennox boys also relocated to Denver, Colorado and established a commonwealth known as the Lennox Denver Pelones, reinforced the propagandist ideology, and began colonizing and socializing local residents that lived in run down communities and public housing units. In general, Los Angeles has an aura of being affluent and glamorous, thus even street gang members are looked at with mysticism and reverence because of their international public image, which intrigues those who are easily influenced because they want to be part of the scene, even though they have never been to Los Angeles. Lennox gang members made several attempts to establish commonwealths in Hollywood, Las Vegas, Phoenix, Denver, and Tijuana, and expand their sphere of influence throughout different territories, yet neither was as successful as in Albuquerque, New Mexico, where they accumulated more land, capital, and labor than in their own fatherland.

In the early 90's, a group of explorers from the street organization of Lennox traveled to Albuquerque, New Mexico, and discovered a poverty-stricken wasteland that had potential for increased GNP (gross national product). There were many low-income residents who had substance abuse problems, but there was not much availability of drug resources and the demand was higher than the supply. The Lennox boys quickly took advantage of the situation and asked the fatherland to send drugs and monies to set up a commonwealth where their profit margin could increase more than 100%. They quickly began accumulating land, capital, labor, and extended their sphere of influence throughout the region and used their propaganda skills for fear and intimidation. As they engaged in foreign direct investment and increased human resources (recruitment and expansion), a struggle for power and wealth developed with competitive rivals, who were predominantly from a black/ crip street gang from Los Angeles known as Rolling 60's. Most street gang organizations from the Los Angeles County are mercantilists because the goals and objectives of state growth, development, and representation are primary to commerce, however they recognize that power is parallel with wealth and they adopt economic/political policies simultaneously for the sovereignty of the state. The Lennox boys, along with other

South Siders that moved to the area, began preparing for urban warfare and began building up their military defense to eliminate healthy competition and create a monopoly in the market. The low-intensity conflict took a turn when the Rolling 60's murdered a South Sider from Temple St, and the conflict turned into a street war that left the South Siders victorious with very little competition. Shot-callers (policy-makers) in Albuquerque were subsidizing individuals who would murder any rival from Rolling 60's and other opposition, thus law enforcement agencies began surveillance and investigation into the operation. As the Lennox boys and other South Siders established power, national security, and domination, an unforeseen event that involved child abuse led investigators to raid known drug houses and they began arresting suspects. One of the first perpetrators to get arrested, cooperated with law enforcement agencies, joined the witness protection program, and snitched on fellow gang members, which resulted in the downfall of the Albuquerque commonwealth. Most of the perpetrators were arrested for racketeering, extortion, murder, attempted murder, drug trafficking, and some received consecutive life sentences and others the death penalty. The trial received international attention and the Lennox boys adopted a new reverence and reputation because of their attempts of imperialism.

During the late 1980's, a wave of immigrants from El Salvador were seeking political refuge in the United States because of a bloody civil war that divided the country. As the children of those immigrants grew up into young adults, the need to create a social contract as a means of protection from street gang organizations and other pressure groups seemed imperative. Most of the Salvadoran immigrants settled in Washington D.C. and Los Angeles, California, in the Downtown/Central Los Angeles regional bloc throughout the Hollywood area where gang activity was running rampant. Throughout the Pico Union district, the 18th St gang controlled the community by intimidating citizens and keeping them in fear and frustration, and many Central American immigrants in the area joined the gang voluntarily and some were "strong-armed." A group of Salvadorans created their own street gang organization known as MS 13, Mara Salvatrucha, to resist other street gang organizations and maintain their sovereignty in a brave new world. Many of them had been guerilla fighters in their home countries and were no strangers to extreme violence, so creating a street gang organization and struggling for power, wealth, and national security seemed like a walk in the park. Many of them had lost their sense of fear and were not afraid of anything because they had been exposed to: police torture, incarceration in a third world country, hardcore criminal activity, military as well as street fighting, and living on the streets; so, gang culture helped provide some sort of fraternity for them that was non-existent. As their socialization within street gang culture increased, they incorporated loathsome methods of torture and murder they had experienced in their home countries, to the urban warfare existing within street gang organizations.

In the early 1990's, the United States government passed an immigration policy that exported gang members that were arrested for criminal activity to their home countries they barely even knew or remembered, because of increased gang violence and lack of prison space. Many of them barely spoke Spanish and were foreigners in their own land, yet they began forming networks of teenagers and young adults who were abandoned, unemployed, and alienated, thus they began exporting the propagandist ideology of Los Angeles street gang culture. Throughout the Central American region, deported street gang members spread the street gang lifestyle, enlisted eager recruits, and easily impressed local residents who secretly coveted living in the United States, specifically in Los Angeles, California, "home of the brash, outrageous, and free." As street gang violence and gang membership increased throughout the Americas, authorities in Guatemala and El Salvador began building and designating prisons just for gang members because of the lack of social infrastructure, resources, and monies, to effectively deal with this sweeping phenomenon. Most of the deported immigrants are from 18th St and MS 13, and through default, they have helped the globalization of street gang organizations and have become a regional hegemony throughout Central America. The geopolitics of MS 13 and 18th St have transcended national borders and the deported gang members are considered displaced personnel and expatriates of street gang organizations in Los Angeles, therefore, they are inadvertently sent to live abroad, look for commercial and criminal opportunities, study foreign languages and cultures, and in essence procure international education and training. MS and 18th St have taken their territorial rivalry from Los Angeles to the Americas; they identify themselves with extreme tattooing of the face, they build international networks through the internet, telecommunications, and other mediums of communication, and are in essence creating a virtual state where much of their influence, power, and wealth, can be obtained from abroad.

Most of the deported gang members have an objective

to get back to the states, specifically to the gang Mecca of Los Angeles, however, because of the harsh crackdowns and pressure from law enforcement agencies, when they return to the country illegally they migrate to the east coast and other parts of the country. These new virtual street gang organizations are more organized and assist fellow gang members with protection, housing, refuge, and commercial/criminal opportunities to facilitate their transitions back or newly arrived into the states. Law enforcement agencies have found MS and 18th St gang members throughout the U.S. including; Maryland, Washington D.C., New York, New Jersey, Florida, N. Carolina, Washington, Colorado, Missouri, Oregon, Idaho, Utah, Arizona, New Mexico, Nebraska, Texas, Oklahoma, Kansas, Minnesota, Iowa, Montana, Louisiana, Arkansas, Tennessee, Kentucky, Illinois, Wisconsin, Michigan, Indiana, Georgia, Virginia, Pennsylvania, Hawaii, Alaska, parts of Canada, and of course throughout Central America.

The Immigration and Customs Enforcement Agency (ICE), which is part of the Department of Homeland Security, rounds up foreign gang members as part of maintaining national security and gang enforcement, and works with law enforcement agencies in Honduras, Guatemala, El Salvador, Mexico, and throughout the states, to discuss techniques about how deportation efforts have not decreased gang membership, and how it has subsequently internationalized street gang organizations. MS and 18th St have moved into other capital-intensive enterprises including; human smuggling of undocumented immigrants, counterfeiting identifications, international arms trafficking, organized drug commerce, and have engaged in much more violent behavior including domestic/international executions and holding residents hostage. Authorities in Central America have adopted an anti-gang policy called "Mano Dura," which is a very draconian policy that incarcerates individuals just for having tattoos or belonging to a gang and has been compared by civil rights advocates to the tortures and murders of the 80's during the civil war in El Salvador. Coincidentally, many prisoners have died because of guard negligence in El Salvador, including two separate prison fires in 18th St and MS cell blocks that left almost two-hundred prisoners dead. As recently as August 2005, in three separate Guatemalan prison riots between 18th St and MS rivals, left at least thirty-one inmates dead. Some inmates had weapons ranging from knives to assault weapons like AK 47's, and in many cases where inmates have died, investigations have concluded that prison guards and faculty were directly responsible. (cnn.com) MS and 18th St have taken their low-intensity street rivalry, into an international high-intensity conflict that transcends national borders, and have helped export street gang phenomenon across the globe and have increasingly reinforced the propagandist ideology.

Chapter 11: The Treaty of the South Side

In the summer of 1993, the South Side Senators decreed a general peace treaty agreement amongst a multitude of street gang organizations, which resulted in a temporary deferral of urban warfare. The Bloods and Crips had declared a peace treaty in 1992, after the Los Angeles riots, and set the precedent for the Treaty of the South Side of Hispanic street gang organizations. The general agreement had been debated and discussed by committees for several months, and once it was ratified it marked the end of an era for the historical context and development of street gang organizations. The chief architects of the general agreement had an economic development/humanitarian agenda for the peace treaty and immediately took action to enforce its protocols.

The basic underlying principle was that if any particular gang undermined the authority of the agreement, repercussions would be suffered by their fellow gang members in prison or on the streets by collective action. This fundamental principle was known as the red light/green light phenomenon, where a red light suggests peace and security, while a green light suggests open season (naked aggression) by a multitude. Once the underground media reported the information to the general public, urban politicians had to hold several press conferences to discuss the basic principles of the peace

treaty, and meetings were held constantly for street gang/
political reeducation. The basic principles included: promoting
peace, security, and economic development, which the
urban politicians of each particular gang had to articulate
and enforce amongst their general public and constituents.
According to the peace agenda, street gang organizations
were not allowed to engage in urban warfare amongst
each other, however they were encouraged and allowed to
declare war against black street gang organizations, and if
any battles materialized with other Hispanic street gangs, they
would have to report it immediately to their city council. The
security agreement maintained that street gang members
could pass through as transients through other neighborhoods
and not suffer repercussions or reprisals, but they had to pass
through with the intent of establishing friendly relations. The
economic development agenda maintained that street gang
organizations should engage in capital-intensive programs
to build up a surplus and increase their GDP, and pay a
federal income tax to the senate as a form of taxation with
representation.

After a few months of political reeducation and
assimilation of the general peace agreement, the South Side
Senate held a meeting in the Elysian Park of East Los Angeles,
known as the Elysian Park Conference, where street gang
organizations from all over Southern California attended
to further discuss the principles of the general agreement.
Throughout the conference, many rival street gangs were
allowed to fight one-on-ones to settle scores and take out their
aggression, although it was monitored by chief participants
of the agreement, and it wasn't allowed to escalate further.
After the basic principles were conveyed to all street gang

organizations in an all-inclusive manner, they broke off into sections according to regional bloc status, and discussed regional goals for achieving cooperation in solving social and economic concerns. It appeared like a scene from the motion picture The Warriors where at least 1000 gang members from all over Southern California convened, including classic rivals standing next to each other, to acquiesce the basic principles of the general agreement. During the conference, the park was surrounded by the LAPD in riot gear, patrol squad cars, helicopters, and officers on foot in case the conference resulted in anarchy; however, the Elysian Park Conference was a success for the general agreement and helped trigger the self-restraint and cooperation of street gang organizations.

The Treaty of the South Side was instrumental in reducing gang violence among Hispanic street gang organizations, however many began channeling their efforts into urban warfare against black street gangs. Many Hispanic street gang organizations did not have a significant black street gang presence throughout their regional bloc or vicinity, so they relaxed a little and built up their military capabilities, capital-intensive

programs, and gross domestic product (GDP). However, other street gang organizations were at a disadvantage, including Hispanic street gang organizations in Compton and South Central where the black street gangs had a significant presence, and engaged in inexorable urban warfare against black street gangs, which resulted in heavy casualties. In the West Side regional bloc, a meeting held at Imperial Beach, which was known as the Imperial Beach Conference, resulted in the cooperation of the West Side street gangs and the promoting of peace, security, and economic development throughout the region. The basic principles and agendas of the general agreement, regional goals, and social/economic concerns were discussed among high-ranking public officials of the West Side and South Side Senators. Other issues included territorial adjustments such as small cliques/gangs being drafted into larger street gang organizations, the coercion and assault on party/tagging crew associations, and urban warfare against black street gangs. Throughout the West Side, the general agreement threatened the sovereignty of small street gang organizations because the chief architects of the peace treaty did not want pockets of small gangs because of accountability, districting, and federal tax regulations, thus many were coerced into larger street gang organizations and some petitioned the decision and were officially recognized as a legitimate gang. For example, MXP (Mexican Power) members were drafted into Lennox during a West Side meeting, Woodtown Posse was drafted into Inglewood, and Criminals 13 which were located in Westchester, were on the verge of being annexed by Lennox at a West Side meeting, but as they were being coerced into incorporation, they resisted the annexation, ran off in retreat, and petitioned the decision and won the right to remain autonomous. Other territorial adjustments included the drafting of tagging/party crew associations because of their volume, therefore many tagging/party crew members accepted the decision, some abandoned their attachment to the association, and some resisted the annexation and started their own street gang organization by petition.

During the Imperial Beach Conference, decision-makers concluded that West Side regional bloc gangs would declare urban warfare on the Venice Shoreline Crips, an active black street gang organization located in the unincorporated community of Venice. The urban warfare was ostensibly an ethnic cleansing because of the heavy casualties suffered by the Shoreline Crips, which were attacked by the street organizations of Venice, Sawtelle, Culver City, and Santa Monica, however the Shoreline Crips retaliated with serious counterattacks that left the West Side in a state of emergency. During a West Side meeting, the Lennox boys were asked for assistance and participation in the warfare against the Shorelines, and as the Lennox street gang organization pondered the distance and involvement, the Venice Shoreline Crips passed through the Lennox neighborhood and caught the Lennox boys by surprise, showed their flag and weapons, and maintained a non-aggression pact with no intentions of warfare. Moreover, this event became the determining factor for the Lennox boys to remain neutral because the Shorelines could have murdered a few of their popular gang members, thus they rejected the offer with justification and sincerity, but worked cooperatively to reach other goals. Although the urban warfare on the West Side increased the death/ incarceration rate for gang members in the region, objective analysts were impressed by the regional cooperation of the West Side regional bloc gangs, which once had perennial rivalries.

Coincidentally, the West Side gangs also worked cooperatively to enhance the region's image by promoting cultural festivals and mega-events to attract public support and tourism, specifically Lennox and Culver City. (See Ch. 12) Along the LAX Airport area, the street gang organization of Lennox had declared urban warfare on small pockets of black street gangs and drug dealers around their neighborhood, which was directly related to the murder of one of their popular and well-revered individuals by the Rolling 60's black street gang organization. While Venice, Culver City, Sawtelle, and Santa Monica were engaged in urban warfare with the Shoreline Crips, and Lennox was engaged in urban warfare with Rolling 60's and Eucalyptus Mob, the Inglewood 13 boys, which were one of the main Hispanic street gangs in the West Side, did not make an effort to declare urban warfare against the significant presence of black street gangs throughout the area including: Crenshaw Mafia, Swans Blood Gang, Inglewood Family, Queen Street Bloods, and Inglewood 111th. As a result, Inglewood 13 was denounced by those in the West Side regional bloc, and they became disassociated with the West Side gangs during the cultural festivals and mega-events of the general peace treaty agreement. The general agreement also allowed for the intensification of drug commerce throughout the West Side because of increased networking, cooperation, and connections developed by the general agreement that helped contribute to the coalition of regional goals, which in turn neglected the principal of national self-determination.

As the general peace treaty agreement progressed and developed, security councils were developed in regional blocs to handle disputes that could threaten the peace accord. Security councils could make recommendations to parties involved in conflicts, use diplomatic measures to resolve disagreements, and after all options had been exhausted and a danger still existed that threatened regional peace, they could impose acts of aggression and take enforcement measures. Temporary green light public policy was implemented when issues could not be resolved through diplomacy, so rival gangs used windows of opportunity to assume aggression. Security councils also imposed the federal taxation for the maintenance and development of the county-wide peace agreement, which became a cumbersome regulation for some street gang organizations.

Throughout the East Los Angeles region, a group of rival factions known as the Maravilla gangs defected from the general peace treaty agreement, which was known as the Maravilla Tax Revolt, and became known as green-light gangsters. Prior to the peace accord, the Maravilla gangs had perennial rivalries; however, after the general peace agreement imposed federal tax regulations, they joined forces and orchestrated a strong united front against all street gang organizations and the South Side Senate. The Maravilla gangs included: Arizona Maravilla, El Hoyo Maravilla, Ford Maravilla, Fraser Maravilla, Gage Maravilla, High Times Maravilla, Juarez Maravilla, Lote Maravilla, Lopez Maravilla, Lomita Maravilla, Marianna Maravilla, Project Boys Maravilla, and Rascals Maravilla. The Maravilla gangs criticized the South Side Senate and the peace treaty because of federal tax regulations, biased public policy including green lights and acts of aggression, and undermining their sovereignty, thus they became a subversive organization. The South Side Senate imposed collective security action against the Maravilla gangs; however it did not deter their subversive behavior and they abandoned their participation in the peace accord. As a result, the green light policy was implemented in County jails throughout Southern California and they were separated from the general population and the gang module and were held under protective custody. However, the green light policy was not implemented in California State prisons because most of the Maravilla prisoners had been incarcerated prior to the general peace agreement, which resulted in a conflict of interest with their representatives on the outside. Throughout the West Side regional bloc, biased public policy resulted in temporary green lights and windows of opportunity and aggression, however some street gang organizations used the peace accord to enhance their image and become Olympic Cities amongst Southern California street gang culture.

Chapter 12: Mega-Event Cities

According to the mega-event strategy, cities compete on the global stage for world attention, tourism, and publicity. In the United States, cities compete for monies and resources from the federal government and their state legislature, thus bidding to host the Olympics is a way to bring prestige to the host city, and compete with world-class cities around the globe. Mega-event cities attract positive attention through media stories surrounding economic development, the mega-event strategy, while creating a tourist bubble. The tourist bubble phenomenon is used for city marketing by creating a tourist destination that generates local tax revenues, including redevelopment in downtown areas that promote the city's cultural events, creating sporting conventions and facilities, and stimulating local businesses and economic growth. In order to actualize the mega-event strategy, these cities rely on public/private partnerships through coalitional power to pursue mega-event strategies and goals to facilitate hosting a prestigious event with as little public controversy and intervention as possible. Informal agreements between politicians and members of the business community play a significant and instrumental role in procuring the bid for the Olympics. This was the case in Los Angeles during the 1984 Olympics when urban politicians used corporate sponsorships to host the mega-event without using public financing. Along with pursuing a redevelopment agenda through economic development, many cities used the mega-event strategy as a way to redefine its image and transform people's perception of the city through a tourist bubble, which serves as a catalyst for urban change.

There are also external conditions that can have a significant impact on pursuing the mega-event strategy which include: natural disasters, international public affairs, terrorist threats, and other current events of the day, nevertheless, hosting a prestigious event like the Olympics is a way to pursue economic development agendas and creates good opportunities for short/long-term tangible/intangible benefits. (Andranovich)

In 1994, the Treaty of the South Side became an external condition that had a significant impact on the way some street gang organizations pursued a redevelopment and economic development agenda. The general peace agreement temporarily deterred urban warfare and promoted regional goals, therefore some neighborhoods saw this as a window of opportunity to promote their street gang organization and capture county-wide positive attention.

In the West Side regional bloc, the Culver City gang used this opportunity to promote the propagandist ideology, and their unconventional lifestyle through the underground media and other tools of communication. Most street gang organizations in Southern California wore the traditional solid dress code/colors that reinforced the propagandist ideology; however the Culver City boys wore red Cincinnati Red's hats, red bandanas, red shoe laces, and other red clothing articles that represented the propagandist ideology, but with more color, which enhanced their public image because of their unconventional approach. On the other hand, when entering the industrial prison complex, the Culver City boys wore the blue flag of the South Side Senators to represent the division of Congress between Northern/Southern California. Throughout the West Side, the Culver City boys had a positive perception because of their lyrical/journalist contributions through the underground media that used pragmatism and creativity. The Culver City underground lyricists formed a partnership with the Sawtelle street gang organization and began promoting the West Side regional bloc as a place to fear and covet simultaneously, through lyrical journalism. Throughout the West Side, the street gang organizations of Culver City, Sawtelle, Santa Monica, and Venice began having cultural festivals known as "West Side Parties" that promoted peace and security throughout the regional bloc, and provided an open platform for lyrical journalists to demonstrate their capabilities.

As the underground media began spreading stories down the coast through the grapevine and the lyrical content reached the unincorporated community of Lennox, those that were part of the progressive movement (See Ch. 13) saw a window of opportunity to promote their street gang organization and their cultural lifestyle. Many of the Lennox liberals that were part of the progressive movement had been socialized in tagging/party crew associations and saw the intangible benefits that hosting a mega-event would bring to their community. The Lennox boys had a negative stigma attached to them because of their significant presence of low-income working class immigrants, and because one of their underground lyricists had a heavy accent, hence they were sometimes denounced as a "wetback gang."

The individuals from the progressive movement, specifically the Jokers clique/political party, understood that hosting a cultural festival would help reinvent their public image through positive county-wide attention, thus they began making preparations to host such an event. They took it up with the city council for discussion and were granted permission to host such an event, however the only provision the city council imposed was that no pubic financing would be used, which subsequently the event coordinators would raise the monies based on their own efforts. They would ultimately be responsible for location, financing, logistics, promotion, and operations, which meant that revenues would be tax-free and the benefits would be intangible and long-term. The redevelopment agenda required the significant presence of the other street gang organizations on the West Side; however the Lennox boys had never been invited to a West Side Party because of the negative stigma attached to their unincorporated community. The West Side cultural festivals included members of Sawtelle, Venice, Santa Monica, and Culver City, which at the time considered themselves the four corners, and excluded other West Side gangs for ideological reasons. The event coordinators spent a significant amount of time distributing publications and promoting their mega-event through the street media, and sent a few diplomats to the Culver City projects with the intent of establishing peaceful relations and an invitation to the festival. Rapport was easily established; coincidentally the Culver City boys were hosting a mega-event that same weekend, but on a different day, and an agreement was reached that they would attend each others' cultural functions.

The Culver City boys used informal agreements with local

residents and members of the business community and held their mega-event in the basketball gymnasium of the Mar Vista Gardens Housing Project, which is located within Culver City, and played host to a prestigious event that rendered positive media recognition. The street gang organization of Lennox sent a convoy to the event as a means of proactive protection, which resulted in over 100 gang members dressed to impress and shattering the negative stigma attached to their organization. The Culver City/Lennox street gang organizations had the most significant presence at the event because of their public image, amount of personnel, median age range, and other demographic factors, which resulted in mutual reverence and admiration that continued throughout the West Side Renaissance. The mega-event was preceded the following day by the cultural festival held in the unincorporated community of Lennox at a private location, which brought back the same group of people and marked the beginning of the cultural Renaissance experienced in the West Side regional bloc during the general peace agreement. The cultural festival was broken up by the Lennox Sheriff, which marched to the private location in riot gear from three different locations, and became overwhelmed by the significant amount of opposite street gang organizations in unison and celebration. Because of the positive media attention and lack of violence, the cultural festival weekend played a historical role in pursuing the mega-event strategy for the Lennox/Culver City street gang organizations, which developed a love/hate relationship, and enjoyed prestigious attention, tourism, and publicity; Lennox and Culver City, a marriage made in the projects.

As the positive publicity of the West Side regional bloc

spread throughout the underground media, a conservative entrepreneur from the Lennox street gang organization formed an informal partnership with a few Culver City boys and other members of the business community, and began pursuing the mega-event strategy using public/private coalitional power to promote regional competitive sport and cultural festivals. Many Culver City boys played football in high school and organized regional sporting events with other West Side gangs, which resulted in increased positive media attention for the region and world-class entertainment for those interested in the street gang culture. Often times, the Lennox street gang organization would host a classic football game between Venice/Culver City, which rendered positive media attention because of their capabilities and perennial rivalry, and drew a large crowd from different regional blocs. When the Culver City boys hosted sporting events in the Mar Vista Gardens Projects, they showed off their urban artwork in the form of graffiti, and it rendered admiration and altered perception because of its precision, style, and dimension, which was associated with social-economic status as mentioned in Chapter 8.

The informal regional partnership used coalitional power and available resources to promote West Side events including festivals and football games through advertisements, word-of-mouth, and distribution of publications, which resulted in mega-event city status for the Lennox/Culver City street gang organizations. Weekends became an opportunity to create a tourist bubble and invent a romanticized image to provide visitors with a pseudo-environment of socio-economic status, fraternity, and subversive, street gang culture excitement. Many locations where constituents of the mega-event cities convened became focal points of interest and tourist destinations for visitors that traveled from different regional blocs and counties that were interested in the lifestyles of the West Side regional bloc gangs. In Culver City, the Mar Vista Gardens Housing Project became a tourist destination for several geographical reasons including: availability of space to host cultural festivals on a regular basis, adequate sporting facilities to host regional competitions, and plenty of unmonitored/unlit streets to engage in criminal activity and commerce.

In the unincorporated community of Lennox, Lennox Park became a tourist destination for after hours events, Inglewood Avenue, which is the focal street in the neighborhood, became a tourist destination for female travelers coming in from out-of-town, Isis Park was known for its availability to host regional sport competitions, and several dead ends served as locations to engage in unconventional activities. Throughout the unincorporated community of Lennox, the tourist bubble helped develop growth for local businesses including: Acosta's Tacos, which stayed open late to cater to the "West Side Party" crowd, Daniel's Barber Shop, which catered to local constituents, and during the cultural renaissance, had an increase in growth due to the prestige brought by the mega-event city status, and Jim's Diner, which had been a local hang-out for Lennox gang members for years, experienced a period of growth due to the tourist bubble phenomenon.

The cultural festivals throughout the West Side regional bloc drew such a large crowd that the public/private partnership, which became an independent committee, assumed responsibility and leadership for the events and created "One Way Productions," and hosted the events in empty warehouses from Santa Monica to Torrance. The West Side Parties also provided a platform for underground lyricists to exhibit their talent and capabilities amongst a multitude, and validate their creative style and methodology.

Style of dress began transforming as gang members from the West Side regional bloc adopted a somewhat "preppy" look that contributed to the cultural renaissance, and helped influence gang members from other areas to transform their dress code to a less conspicuous and intimidating look.

As the cultural festivals developed and progressed, physical altercations and disagreements between different gangs became more commonplace, and temporary green lights were imposed sporadically, which allowed rival gangs windows of opportunity to assume aggression. The West Side cultural festivals came to a climax at a Gardena warehouse where the street gang organizations of Lennox/Gardena were involved in a physical altercation that left individuals of both gangs hospitalized with bullet wounds, which contributed to temporary urban warfare between Lennox and Gardena that lasted for months and led to a few murders. The Lennox/Culver City relationship had been so well-established, that when the physical altercation between Lennox/Gardena began, the Culver City gang assisted the Lennox boys and drove one of their members that suffered a bullet wound to the hospital, which continued the reciprocity of admiration and reverence for one another, and lasted for a few years until it reached its climax.

The Lennox/Culver City street gang organizations were directly responsible for the West Side renaissance, and how the regional bloc flourished during the Treaty of the South Side. Hosting a mega-event on the same cultural festival weekend resulted in a friendly relationship based on admiration and reverence; however, the relationship was often compromised by personal conflict and ambiguity. At the beginning of the relationship, both street organizations entertained each other in their respective neighborhoods and hosted each other in different focal points that would later become target destinations during temporary conflicts. As the regional bloc attracted positive media attention, the Lennox/Culver City street gang organizations spent a significant amount of time in each other's neighborhoods that was unprecedented in street gang history, and was directly related to their mega-event city status.

During the West Side Renaissance, it was commonplace for the Lennox boys to hang out in the Culver City projects during after hours and regional sporting activities, similarly the Culver City boys would write Culver City/Lennox 13 on public/private surfaces and hold private parties in Lennox territory. The relationship extended outside of the regional bloc and carried over to other popular and street gang cultural activities including: specific dance clubs, cars shows, popular ethnic festivals, street cruising, bars, and long weekend holidays celebrated in Ensenada, Tijuana, and Rosarito, Mexico. When they would see each other at these types of events and activities, they would establish rapport, stay close to each other, carry on with whatever they were doing, and keep a watchful eye just in case trouble unraveled, and have each others' backs when fights would break out.

On one occasion that marked the depth of their relationship, the Lennox/Culver City street gang organizations attended a Car Show in the Los Angeles Coliseum that attracted county-wide street gang organizations. During a musical performance by a Los Angeles-based rap group, street gang organizations and fans in the audience threw their hands in the air and applauded the performer's capabilities and efforts, and in turn the Culver City boys began waving their red bandanas/Cincinnati Reds hats in the air because of their patriotism and representation of their neighborhood. Other street gang organizations in the audience began denouncing and plotting against the Culver City gang because their red urban apparel was associated with the Nortenos, (street gang organizations in Northern California that are directly responsible for the polarization of the Prison Congress) and walked out of the stadium to wait for the Culver City boys and began to conspire. The Culver City boys looked at the Lennox boys and instantly knew that they had their backs and walked out in unison with more than 100 gang members ready to embark into a battle zone; however, the conspirators were overwhelmed by the amount of personnel and their eagerness to engage in a physical altercation. Through diplomatic and uncompromising efforts, the West Side regional bloc gangs were able to uphold their patriotism and representation of the regional bloc, while maintaining their defiance against the status-quo.

Despite the affinity and rapport that was established between the Lennox/Culver City street gang organizations, personal conflicts of interest between individual gang members resulted in temporary battles that compromised their relationship. Personal conflicts involving women, drugs, pride, patriotism, and other miscellaneous reasons resulted in feuds that started between two individuals that forced the entire gang to follow suit reluctantly. The love/hate relationship lasted for a few years until it reached its climax in 1997 at a private cocktail party in a Culver City bar, where a gathering of women, Culver City boys, and Lennox gang members, resulted in absolute chaos. The night was progressing relatively smoothly, until a disagreement unfolded between a Culver City boy, his girlfriend, and two Lennox gang members, which involved the girlfriend making accusations against the Lennox boys stealing her purse. The Culver City boys utilized diplomacy to diffuse the situation, however, the mutual hostility had been building up and once the first punch was thrown, it turned into a bloodbath that involved bottles, pool sticks, and liquor glasses. As the battle zone moved outdoors, the Culver City Police Department observed, without preventing the animosity, which resulted in a Culver City boy being shot and paralyzed, a high speed pursuit, and the incarceration and hospitalization of a few Lennox gang members. The event was discussed at a West Side regional bloc Security Council meeting, and it marked the end of the regional cooperation, West Side Renaissance, and love/hate relationship between Culver City/Lennox. Although the friendly relations between West Side regional bloc gangs was severed, the West Side Renaissance rendered mega-event city status for the West Side regional bloc, specifically Lennox and Culver City, which for a few years they enjoyed prestigious county-wide attention, tourism, and publicity.

Chapter 13: The Progressive Movement

In the early 20th century, a political movement known as the Progressive Movement transformed government structures with new ideas about organization and administration. Going against the status-quo, the Progressive Movement attracted disillusioned groups and individuals that were excluded and ignored by the leadership group, and engaged in unorthodox political behavior and ideas that helped influence the reformation of government. The Progressive Movement based their philosophy on four key paradigms that included: 1. pragmatic optimism, in which individuals succumbed to humanism and could alter the ecology of their environments. 2. Scientific management, which included budgeting and business ideas that adopted efficiency, effectiveness, and economy for organization and management. 3. An emphasis on the utilitarianism and the welfare of the citizenry, rather than cultural or religious attachments. 4. Lastly, government bureaucracies run by well-educated elites and those that have had successful achievements in business and the private sector.

Progressive thinkers believed that government leadership, power, laws, and the welfare of the community could best be achieved by having those with the most knowledge, skills, and abilities perform civil duties that the average person wasn't capable of administering. The Progressive Movement transcended political parties and paradigms and maintained that effective governance can be achieved through project development and public policy that is reflective of the citizenry, and provides for the welfare of the community. What resulted from the Progressive Movement was the idea to constantly reinvent government organization and administration through systematic efficiency, and private-sector business practices like privatization. (Saltzstein) In the unincorporated community of Lennox, the Progressive Movement sought to radically transform government organization and administration, but it resulted in warring factions that were directly responsible for the fall of the empire.

In the early 1980's, a group of individuals from a party crew known as "Insanity Boys" congregated around 111th St. and Firmona Avenue, in the unincorporated community of Lennox. The Insanity Boys were known for by reputation and popularity amongst other party crews, women, for their break-dancing skills, thus the gang members around the community observed them as a potential threat to their sovereignty. As the popularity and reputation of the Insanity Boys increased, the Lennox boys' tolerance decreased, and they began coercing the Insanity Boys into the street gang organization of Lennox. The Insanity Boys acquiesced and adopted a clique/political party known as the "Night Owls," which was a separatist clique/political party that was against the status-quo, and was the first wave of Lennox liberals that were part of the progressive movement. The new Night Owls click served as agents of change for the street gang organization of Lennox and had different ideas about organization and administration, thus the conservative gang members viewed them as anti-patriotic and radical. The Night Owls were an elitist party that allowed for minimal partisanship and recruitment, therefore some of the Lennox conservatives picked fights and began party-bickering (clique-tripping) because of their unconventional practices. These practices included a different style of dress such as: white slip-on Vans, corduroy Levis, and Hawaiian pattern button shirts, which was unusual for street gang members in those days. They congregated in a location that was away from traditional Lennox boy hang outs, which was at a dead-end street on Mansel Avenue known as the Night Owl nest, and they rarely congregated with other Lennox boys at conventions and parties. They were an elitist unit that sought reformation of street gang ideology, they were young, good-looking, had money, and had an impressive reputation with women. They put in a lot of work for their neighborhood on enemy rivals, and they were not afraid of the conservative faction that existed within their street gang organization, but instead they welcomed with open fists. What resulted were small pockets of civil unrest within the unincorporated community of Lennox, which included fist fights, rumbles, and shootings, between the Lennox liberals and conservatives that resulted in warring factions amongst themselves.

As the reputation of the Night Owls increased, a second wave of young liberals began emerging and developing the same progressive movement philosophy. Because the Night Owls' membership was becoming overwhelming, a new political party was created to account for the second wave of the progressive movement. During the late 80's, a handful of moderate Night Owls began a clique/political party known as the Pee Wee Locos, which they founded, and recruited the young liberals who had expressed interest and admiration for the progressive movement. Many of the Pee Wee Locos had relatives that belonged to the Night Owls, however unlike the Night Owls, they did not come from a party crew and they congregated with those of the conservative right, bridging somewhat of a gap between liberalism and conservatism.

Coincidentally, some of the Night Owls began seeing the Pee Wee Locos as a threat to their sovereignty and reputation because they began stealing the spotlight, subsequently party bickering followed, which were the first signs of a divided progressive movement. Fights broke out between the Night Owls and Pee Wee Locos, which rendered a positive reputation for the Pee Wee Locos because they stood up to the more experienced gang members and they maintained their ground. Nevertheless, the Pee Wee Locos maintained the reputation of the progressive movement, which included being young, good-looking, having a positive reputation amongst women and rival enemies, and having money, but they abandoned the extreme polarities of the ideological spectrum for the sake of utility. Moreover, because of their moderate philosophy, they were not entirely against the status-quo, they did not seek reformation of ideology or dress code, they were not that elitist, yet they were involved in party-bickering (clique-tripping) with a faction from the conservative right. The Pee Wee Locos served as change agents for the unincorporated community of Lennox because the progressive movement started becoming polarized, it started becoming more attractive to moderates, and the status-quo began adopting elements of liberalism and conservatism. They had their headquarters on Felton Avenue and congregated with liberals and conservatives. They were the first group of gang members in the unincorporated community of Lennox to shave their heads and wear Le Tigre polo shirts, which was unconventional for street gang members at that time. The progressive movement had appeared to have been co-opted by the conservatives, which neutralized the radical fervor of the Lennox liberals, yet a new group of individuals from the Mexican Power clique emerged and helped transform the street gang organization of Lennox to continue the legacy of the progressive movement.

During the late 1980's, the third wave of Lennox liberals from the progressive movement emerged from a loose coalition of disillusioned individuals, who came from tagging/party/ and dance crews known as: HNR (Hit n Run), After Hours, and The Wanderers. This group of individuals was much more unconventional than the previous wave of the progressive movement, which included style of dress and music they adopted from Joy Division, The Smiths, The Cure, Bauhaus, and other such gothic/dark wave/new wave music from the British pop scene. They incorporated the British pop culture with their Mexican American identities, and produced positive underground media attention and influence amongst some younger groups of individuals, women, and the traditional gang members from the unincorporated community of Lennox. Like disillusioned and isolated teenagers growing up anywhere in the world, they were dealing with the macrocosmic problem of an identity crisis and a social paradox of existence. They were trying to get the balance right between graffiti, music, ethnicity, and fashion trends they considered, which fit parallel to the music they adopted. When this unconventional group of individuals reached high school, their positive reputations, eclecticism, and trend-setting behavior followed them, thus they drew a bigger crowd that extended from Lennox to Lawndale. During a high school dance for a Cinco De Mayo celebration, a group of black high school students that were wearing black power medallions (Yo' MTV Raps had popularized African medallions during the late 1980's) were denouncing the ethnic celebration, which directly led to this coalition of individuals to adopt the name "Mexican Power" as a form of empowerment, to demonstrate nationalism and solidarity. As a consequence, a riot followed between Mexican American and African American students. This marked the beginning of the Mexican Power ideology, and ethnic riots across different high school campuses that Mexican Power boys attended. As their reputation for ethnic solidarity and riot-inciting increased, their membership increased exponentially due to their positive underground media attention and their reputable image that transcended convention. For example; many of them dressed like rock-n-roll greasers/punk rockers which earned them the name of the hippie locos, many dressed really sporty with baseball caps, Colorado boots, cross trainers, and casual jeans, while others dressed like liberal or conservative street gang members.

The Mexican Power faction came from different cultural socializations, but they worked effectively to achieve their mission statement, which included ethnic nationalism and solidarity, and progressive movement values. Party identification and demographics transcended Mexican ethnicity and included members from different backgrounds including: Columbian, Argentinean, Peruvian, Caucasian, Puerto Rican, and others. Many adopted street gang pseudonyms, some kept their graffiti pseudonym, and many others used both a street gang and graffiti pseudonym to carry on their reputation. When one of the main Mexican Power boys wrote his graffiti name in the Lennox territory on public surfaces in street gang wild style, many young graffiti writers were immediately drawn to the organization, however the Lennox gang members saw it as a threat to their sovereignty. The Mexican Power boys popularized a dead end street (Truro Ave.) in the unincorporated community of Lennox, and began drawing some of the Lennox liberals from the progressive movement, including the Pee Wee Locos and Night Owls, which respectively earned them the same rivals. As their reputation in the underground media increased, many Lennox liberals/conservatives tried pressuring MXP boys into their street gang organization, however they wanted to remain autonomous and found themselves constantly having to fight and prove themselves against the Lennox boys. When the MXP boys entered the industrial prison complex, they claimed Lennox as their sovereignty due to prison politics, yet when they returned to the streets, they upheld their faction as their absolute sovereignty. As the Truro dead end became more infested with Lennox liberals and conservatives, the MXP boys vanished from the area and spread to different pockets of hang outs in the South Bay between Lennox and Lawndale. They were no longer a significant threat to the street gang organization of Lennox, and their sphere of influence began diminishing when some of the main protagonists were murdered and incarcerated, thus a new group of Lennox liberals assumed the responsibility of the progressive movement.

Growing up in the West Side regional bloc of the Los Angeles County in the 80's was an interesting time for Mexican American teenagers from Santa Monica to Redondo Beach. The proximity of the ocean and the cosmopolitan neighborhoods allowed these teenagers to develop their faculties much more radically than their counterparts in South Central, the Valleys, and East L.A. Naturally, they became influenced by the beach culture, affluence, graffiti, hip hop/ gangster rap, ethnic identity, and the ecology of their environment. In the unincorporated community of Lennox, a group of individuals from the Lennox Middle School were riding Santa Cruz skateboards, BMX freestyle bikes, writing their graffiti crew/name on public/private surfaces and on RTD buses, wearing Dogtown/T&C Surf shirts, Vision Gator/Off the Wall Vans, Creepers and tapered Dickies, listening to British pop/underground & hip hop/gangster rap music, and they were practicing dance routines for the local dances/parties. Sometimes, they would ride their bikes and skateboards with backpacks full of spray-paint, mean streaks, and markers to Imperial Beach. There they'd ride waves on their body boards, than tag up graffiti landmarks with their writing tools. Some of these kids would practice dancing routines to underground/ popular dance music to prepare to battle kids at local dances and the cafeteria lunch line. Some put on a Depeche Mode cover band and pretended to be in concert or recording a video, or sometimes they would ride the bus to Hollywood to collect postcards, posters, t-shirts, and imported singles from the Cure, the Smiths, Echo & the Bunnymen, and other British pop music. During their last year attending Lennox Middle School, they organized a crew called "the Peruchi Posse," which was involved in junior high walk-outs, harmless thieving, and they developed a game that involved extreme physical contact, which contained elements of football, rugby, and wrestling. That game developed into an organization they coined "LWF", Lennox Wrestling Federation, which involved personal wrestling matches, tag-team matches, battle royals/

rumbles, and championship belts. These were usually recorded on video, which still circulate in the Lennox underground today. Some of the individuals from the Lennox street gang organization infrequently tried to pressure them into the gang or simply punk them, however, they posed no significant threat to their sovereignty and they were left to their own devices.

As they reached and attended different high schools, these individuals went in different directions including: joining Lennox or MXP, the rival faction of Tepa, party crews, tagging associations, emo-rock bands, and jock groups. Some of the main individuals were from a popular and cosmopolitan tagging association known as FSK (Fuck Society Kings), which after a few years of existence became more territorial and reckless. Simultaneously, some of the FSK members maintained a dual sovereignty with the MXP political party, which in turn rendered an underground graffiti/hip hop culture mentality, combined with a liberal street gang organization ideology. During a transient visit to the Roadium Swap Meet in Gardena, some of the FSK/MXP boys had a run in with a rival tagging association called (KAK), who were known to run with the Compton Barrio 70's gang. This confrontation resulted in a stabbing and incarceration for attempted murder, for one of the FSK/MXP boys. This event benchmarked the beginning of their tag-banging philosophy, which emphasized a specific look and a liberal ideology, along with an infamous underground reputation that separated them from other groups of individuals. Simultaneously, some of their counterparts from the Lennox Middle School had developed a party crew called Tres Equis (Triple X Crew) that engaged in sporting activities and partying events, which also emphasized a specific look and liberal ideology. Accordingly, they began to frequent hang-outs and events collectively, and consequently adopted the same tagging/party crew rivals, which the Lennox street gang organization began viewing as a potential platoon for the next wave of the progressive movement.

The city commissioner and other city council members decided that the FSK and Tres Equis boys would be drafted, and this fourth wave of Lennox liberals was too voluminous to circulate amongst other political parties, thus they revived and old clique called the "Jokers", and made proper accommodations for their acclamation including: weapons, monies, and drugs. As they began to assimilate into the cultural organization of Lennox, they had to prove themselves like the rest of the political parties from the progressive movement and succumb to the contemporary political behavior of the day. Most of the constituents of the Joker's political party had prior experience with: drug experimentation, debauchery, violent/reckless behavior, enemy rivalries, vandalism, grand theft auto, and bravado attitudes. Thus, the transition into the Lennox social contract went relatively smoothly. Many individuals from other political parties wanted to join the Joker's clique, but like their progressive movement predecessors, membership was elitist and selective in order to maintain party identification. Although the Joker's clique were Lennox liberals and part of the progressive movement, they congregated with members from all parties including: Night Owls, Pee Wee Locos, MXP's, Tiny Locos, Hollywood Bandits, Winos, and Tokers. They also frequented others' headquarters and set up their own at Buford Avenue, which some called Joker town. They posted up at a different location on the focal street of Inglewood Avenue, which became popularized during the West Side Renaissance and housed progressive movement members from the conservative right and liberal left.

Some party-bickering developed between the Jokers/MXP due to their previous association and passing of the torch, however peaceful relations outweighed isolated incidents that were mostly individual-specific. As they began to assimilate into their new socialization, their infamous reputation throughout the underground street media increased, the general peace treaty agreement developed and prevented urban warfare, which stigmatized them as "peace-treaty gangsters." Fortunately, the general peace agreement allowed them to pursue their liberal and flexible ideology, while going against the status-quo. This enabled them to maintain their reputation in the underground street media by representing the neighborhood during consistent traveling that included: car shows, cruising, clubbing, partying, shopping, and international getaways. They were known as trouble-makers and had consistent run-ins with rivals that rendered temporary urban warfare. They reacted during green light policies, they were usually responsible when green lights were imposed on the Lennox gang, and when the peace accord declared war with black street gang organizations, they were the first to assassinate a known drug dealer in their neighborhood, which allowed them to take over that business and pursue capital-intensive programs.

Like their predecessors, the Jokers had a specific look that was unconventional for street gang members at the time including: Reebok classics, basketball/running sneakers, Timberland shoes/boots, Lucky Brand and Guess jeans, Polo hats/shirts, baseball caps, baseball batting gloves, and other sporty apparel. They were more stylish and fashionable than their predecessors, other political parties, and rival enemies, thus they dressed for ornamentation and emphasized appearance over utility, which was typical of Parliamentary France. When the general peace treaty agreement took the Los Angeles County by storm, they helped influence the radical transformation of the West Side regional bloc with the West Side Renaissance, and served as agents of change for the unincorporated community of Lennox. The street gang organization of Lennox underwent a cultural makeover that overwhelmed some of the conservative right, which tried to pass public policies that de-emphasized aesthetic dress, which some believed, reduced the infamous reputation of the entire Lennox organization. After a few years of acclimating into their ecological/sociological environment, they became more comfortable with their progressive movement values, thus party-bickering began with a conservative faction that was almost predictable due to the pattern of Lennox liberals. The pattern of warring factions in the unincorporated community of Lennox was directly related to class conflict, which was examined in Ch 6 and divided the street gang organization due to party identification.

The West Side Renaissance allowed many Lennox liberals, moderates, and conservatives, to pursue capital-intensive programs and economic policies due to the temporary deferral of urban warfare, thus a handful of city council members engaged in venture capitalism. Simultaneously, some individuals from the Joker's clique and other parties pursued liberal arts through urban artwork in the form of lyricism, graffiti artwork, and college educations. During the West Side Renaissance, a group of unconventional troubadours started a rap crew called the Post-Meridians that included members from: the Jokers, Tokers, Pee Wee Locos, tagging crew associations, and independent individuals. (See Ch. 10) Throughout the underground media they were called the Mexican Wu-Tang because of their volume and murderous lyricism that transcended orthodox gangster rap, hip hop, and Mexican-American lyricists. The members who made up the venture capitalists and liberal arts circle transcended party identification and had individual-specific clique-tripping with members from other parties including: Jokers, MXP, Night Owls, Pee Wee Locos, Winos, and Tokers. Overall, the contemporary progressive movement transcended party identification and included radical socialists from the extreme left, swing moderates at the center, conservative liberals, and venture capitalists from the extreme right, until a known dictator who had just served a congressional term was released from prison and was directly related to the fall of the empire.

During the first wave of the progressive movement, a fearless intimidator from the Night Owls emerged with a dictatorial and authoritative leadership role to assume power. Members from all political parties, transients, thugged-out residents living in the community, innocent bystanders, and objective analysts feared his presence because his reputation had implored the power of myth. He had impressive knowledge, skills, and abilities in typical street gang culture including: drug commerce, pugilism, consistent work (gang-banging) ethic, street-fighting, debauchery, and congressional terms, thus he used his resume advantageously to pursue leadership theory. He continuously engaged in party-bickering, individual pressuring, personal duels, and recidivism, therefore, most of the members from the street gang organization preferred he remained in prison serving out congressional terms. After serving out a few years in different state institutions, this known dictator was released during the climax of the West Side Renaissance and immediately began gathering intelligence on members from the liberal arts and venture capitalist circle that made up the progressive movement. He immediately began running with the progressive movement and began collecting and gathering empirical evidence on criminal activity.

It wasn't long before he began pressuring, intimidating, and sending individuals on missions to prove their loyalty to the absolute sovereignty of Lennox, however, his information-seeking behavior began raising skepticism amongst a group of individuals from the progressive movement that began plotting out an insurgency group. The insurgency group began when there was a historical fall out between two popular individuals from the progressive movement that left one of them physically injured, which caused an extreme polarization between the progressive movement. One of those members was a main figure head within the venture capitalist circle; therefore his closest allies and he became isolated from the majority of the progressive movement and the rest of the street gang organization. This isolation was directly related to the scandalous methodology used during the infamous fall out and on previous incidents, and the group's extreme abuse of power, physical discipline, and extortion. Coincidentally, many members from the progressive movement began getting busted for engaging in criminal activities which seemed highly suspect that law enforcement would have gathered intelligence, unless there was an informant. The insurgency group had speculated that this dictatorial leader from the Night Owls was an informant for law enforcement agencies, thus when the underground media reported this information as confidential and accurate, the assumption had been confirmed. As the insurgent group began making military preparations for the removal of the dictatorship, a physically abusive altercation between the dictator and a popular member from the progressive movement accelerated the agenda. What resulted was a military coup that removed the dictator from authority and two main members from the insurgency, who were part of the liberal arts Joker's clique serving out a voluntary manslaughter prison term. It engendered disillusionment of most of the street gang organization, and the fall of the empire. Moreover, the dictatorship was never replaced by a peaceful or democratic regime, it disenfranchised and isolated many individuals, and resulted in massive abandonment of the social contract.

Epilogue

In 1998, N.W.A. (Niggaz with Attitude), internationalized the Los Angeles street gang culture when they released a subversive rap album that captured the essence of the regional urban struggle. Because of their controversial lyrics and observable display of the street gang dress code, the rap group was embraced by inner city youth across the world, but denounced by the popular media and conservative thinkers. Many that identified with the urban struggle all over the country adopted the dress code and helped reinforce the propagandist ideology of the street gang culture. This marked the beginning of gangster rap which began its sphere of influence in the music industry because it was now becoming marketable, and record companies could sell the image. During the early 90's, the music industry became saturated with gangster rap and white, middle-class, suburban kids stimulated record sales by mass purchasing, however, the street gang dress code was considered subversive and mostly accessible to blacks and Hispanics.

Also during the 90's, there was a significant increase in gang membership throughout the Los Angeles County, which directly contributed to the increase in criminal and gang activity. The Peace Treaties of Southern California saw a temporary deterrence of urban warfare; however, this phenomenon did not decrease recruitment and enlistment into street gang organizations. Criminal and gang activity in the West Side regional bloc began to decrease in the late 90's after gang injunctions had been implemented and allowed for high-income residents to move westward and increase property values within the region. Although there were several state-sponsored areas in the West Side where many Hispanics and blacks lived, a 1997 U.S. Housing and Urban Development regulation pushed minorities east, raised rents, and began the gentrification process in the West Side. The West Side experienced an influx of non-organic residents, and significant decrease in minority residents, which has extended to areas like: Silver Lake, Echo Park, Eagle Rock, and Highland Park. These areas were in the process of becoming hipster communities where the residents are no longer organic and drive around in their out-of-state Volvos, Jettas, and Saabs. These hipsters are health-conscious and consume organic products, they drink coffee and hang out in outdoor cafes, and they set local fashion trends in areas like the Sunset Junction. The gentrification process was positively correlated with gang injunctions and the decrease of gang activity within these newly developed hipster communities.

The street gang organization dress code and artwork has been co-opted by popular culture and has changed the physical appearance of the Southern California look. This has been directly related to a well-known tattoo artist, Cartoon from San Pedro, who in the late 90's launched a clothing line called Joker clothing and began tattooing famous rappers. With help from rap moguls Cypress Hill and Psycho Realm, the clothing line emphasized street gang dress code, and their look popularized street gang collages and tattoos. As Cartoon's popularity increased, celebrities began setting up appointments and waiting for months to pay top dollars for prison-style tattoos. Cartoon recently landed a deal with Nike and Vans that allowed him to design a shoe that incorporates traditional street gang artwork. With help from the popular Grand Theft Auto video games as well, the street gang dress code became popularized and co-opted by the masses including white, suburban, middle-class kids. The punk rock gangster look that began in Venice Beach during the late 70's created by Dogtown skaters, was revived in the beginning of the 21st century due to the revival of the skating phenomenon and recent films. Ironically, the street gang organization dress code that was once used as an antisocial propagandist ideology that gang members died for has now become co-opted by the masses and neutralized by popular culture.

References

Abramowitz, A. (2004) Voice of the People: Elections and Voting in the United States. New York: McGraw-Hill.

Bair, L. (1974) The Essential Rousseau. New York: The New American Library Inc.

Bowman, A. O., & Kearney, R.C. (2003) State and Local Government, the Essentials. Boston: Houghton Mifflin Company.

Burbank, M.J., Andranovich, G.D., Heying, C.H. et al. (2001) Olympic Dreams Colorado: Lynne Rienner Publishers Inc.

Daraul, A. (1961) Secret Societies. London: The Octagon Press Ltd.

Jillson, C. (1999) American Government: Political Change and Institutional Development. Texas: Harcourt Brace & Company.

Kegley, C.W., & Wittkopf, E.R. (1988) The Global Agenda: Issues and Perspectives. New York: McGraw-Hill.

Korey, J.L. (2002) California Government: Third Edition. Boston: Houghton Mifflin Company.

McLuhan, M. (1964) Understanding Media: The Extensions of Man. New York: McGraw-Hill.

Newcomer, O. (1993) Governing Los Angeles. New York: McGraw-Hill.

Saltzstein, A.L. (2003) Governing America's Urban Areas. California: Wadsworth/Thomson Learning Inc.

Schneider, H.W. (1958) Leviathan Parts I and II. Indianapolis: Bobbs-Merrill Educational Publishing.

Walker, S.L. (2004) A Vicious Cycle. *Daily Breeze*. A1-A15.

Wayne, S.J. (2003) Is This Any Way to Run a Democratic Election? Boston: Houghton Mifflin Company.